Mistake Free Medical Office Design *and* Construction

MISTAKE FREE MEDICAL OFFICE DESIGN and CONSTRUCTION

Written Exclusively for Physicians & Dentists

Richard Boureston

SCMRE Publishing
Irvine, California

Mistake Free Medical Office Design and Construction, by Richard Boureston

Published by:
SCMRE Publishing
5500 Trabuco Rd.
Suite 100
Irvine, CA 92620

Copyright © 2009 by Richard Boureston

All rights reserved. No part of this book may be reproduced or transmitted in any form or by any means, electronic or mechanical, including photocopying, recording, or by any information storage and retrieval system without written permission from the publisher, except for the inclusion of brief quotations in a review.

ISBN–13: 978–0–9823195–1–2

Cover & Interior Design: Desktop Miracles, Inc.

Publisher's Cataloging-In-Publication Data
(Prepared by The Donohue Group, Inc.)

Boureston, Richard.
   Mistake free medical office design and construction / written exclusively for physicians & dentists [by] Richard Boureston.
     p. ; cm.
   Includes index.
   ISBN: 978-0-9823195-1-2

    1. Medical offices—Design and construction. 2. Dental offices—Design and construction. 3. Medical offices—Planning. 4. Dental offices—Planning. I. Title.
R728 .B68 2009
                                                  725.23

Printed in the United States of America

Acknowledgments

Like all worthy endeavors we pursue in life, we often look to others for encouragement and aide. This project was no different. I must first thank Ken McCarthy and Howie Jacobson for encouraging me to write this book. I also thank the many doctors I spoke with over the years for taking time to share their experiences with me. A special thanks to Dr. Ken Tokita, Dr. Richard Harder DDS, Dr. Bruce Albert, Dr. Albert Fuchs, Dr. Todd Miller DDS, Dr. Sam Sunshine, Dr. John Cheng, Dr. Harpreet Bawa DDS and her husband Rantandeep Bawa, Wayne Edwards, Ron Sakahara, Omar Franco, Steve Sunshine, and Ed Nance, all who contributed to the success of this book.

    I must also thank my father for inviting me to join him in this adventure called commercial real estate, my mother for her support, and my wife and children for enduring the long hours necessary to complete this project. Most importantly, I must acknowledge that without God's grace in my life and His willingness to sustain me I could do nothing.

About the Author

Richard Boureston joined The Boureston Companies in 1998. He has developed nearly 1,000,000 square feet of medical office space and specializes in consulting for doctors and investors and developing medical office buildings and hospitals. He maintains a blog at medicalrealestate.wordpress.com.

Contents

Acknowledgments   5
About the Author   7
Introduction   11

CHAPTER ONE	Finding Medical Office Space	17
CHAPTER TWO	Negotiating the Deal	41
CHAPTER THREE	Financing	61
CHAPTER FOUR	Space Planning and Construction Drawings In 3 Months or Less	79
CHAPTER FIVE	Construction	93
CHAPTER SIX	Operating Your Business	113
CHAPTER SEVEN	Marketing	139

Index   165

Introduction

I grew up in real estate development. It was what my father did (and does) for a living. After college, I went my own way for a while but eventually joined him in his work and have found I love it. We've developed a specialty in medical office property, and I find this area to be particularly interesting. It is like no other property development we do; learning about the needs of medical providers has been fascinating, and helping physicians and dentists launch their careers—the people who help us stay well and who care for us when we are not—has been especially gratifying work.

My father was born into a lower-middle-class family in the mid-1940s as World War II was ending. His father had lived through the depression and valued stability. As work became available, his father (my grandfather) decided to join the postal service, where he worked for 25 years. At the age of 55, he decided to become a pastor and serve the remaining part of his life ministering to others, particularly to those in senior housing.

As my father grew up, his family frequently gathered with local relatives and during these times he would meet with his great uncle, a successful real estate businessman who encouraged him to go to school and get a college degree, and in particular, to go to the University of Southern California (USC). My father greatly looked up to his great uncle and, ultimately, did graduate from USC with a degree in accounting. He worked in accounting for nearly five years, and held several positions in large companies, including Prudential. But, because of the inspiration of his great uncle, my father always had his eye on real estate development. He was able to fulfill that vision in 1978, when he completed his first project.

Since then, he's continued building his business—and over the course of the past thirty years has become a very successful real estate developer in Orange County and Los Angeles. During that time, as his great uncle got older and was unable to manage the day-to-day operations of his properties, my father began helping manage those properties as well, which he continued to do until his great uncle's death.

In the 1990s, after the recession, my father invited me to join the company. I have become the third generation of real estate business people in my family. My brother joined us five years ago and quickly has become an important asset to the company. As I grew in the business and learned more and more, I was soon given the responsibility of managing the tenant improvements for all the projects that we had constructed. Of course, I made several mistakes along the way—walls in the wrong places, not following up on consultants, not recognizing the details that mattered, not understanding who's responsible for what.

The benefit of managing tenant improvements is that you get to do several projects within one building. Frequently, we would have fifteen to twenty tenants in a building, and I would manage each of those projects. During the time that we were building-out tenant improvements, we were able to ensure that the projects got done quickly, proficiently, and cost effectively. By doing numerous projects over the course of several years in several buildings, I was able to repeatedly go through the construction process, learn from the tenants, and learn what were effective ways to manage the process (and the ineffective ways as well). This was important training for me when I later moved on to managing shell projects and, ultimately, to acquiring land and doing my own medical office building developments.

Tenant improvements are a mini-development project. Instead of using land as your base, you're using an existing building, but the process isn't dissimilar to a large building; there are actually several similar elements that play a role in a successful project. The hundreds of tenant improvements that I've designed, planned, managed, and executed have taught me what can't be acquired any other way. And that's the invaluable experience and information that I'm going to be sharing with you in this book.

While the overall process is quite complex, there is a simple thread that runs through the entire development: people have responsibilities. Each player has a certain scope of work that he or she is responsible for, including the city, the inspectors, the contractor, the architects—all of them have different roles. It becomes far easier to manage the process when you know to whom you should direct your questions, and who to talk to when there's a problem. If it takes you three days to figure out whom you should be talking to, *and* you're trying to run your practice, the project can quickly become overwhelming. Additionally, you need to ensure that the people who have these responsibilities are doing *what* they say they are going to do, *when* they say they are going to do it; follow up becomes very important. These are just some of the things you are going to learn as you go through this book.

Eight years ago we got a call from a broker about a great property next to Irvine Medical Center. At the time, we had done one other medical building several years prior, which was part of a larger retail center and office project. That project was located in a neighborhood and was so desirable to St. Joseph Hospital, they ultimately took the space (and they are still located in that space today). The space next to the Irvine Medical Center was particularly important because of the site's proximity to the hospital and the hospital's desire to contribute property toward the project and feed us the doctors we needed to fill the project.

Of course, none of this came for free. One of the things the hospital required was the right to approve or disapprove each doctor that came into our project, in exchange for their property. So, it became a condition of the lease that any doctor that wanted to lease a space in our building had to get the approval of the hospital first.

As we began the process of constructing the building, we quickly learned that our projections had been correct. We began receiving proposals from the top dentists in the area. Several of these dentists already had existing practices for over ten or fifteen years, and were willing to move their practices into our building because they liked the professional element of being in a medical building as well as the environment of having several dentists together in the same building.

We also found that several of the top doctors in the area wanted to locate themselves near the hospital. Obviously, some of the doctors interested in this location were those that were going to use the hospital's facilities, but there were plenty of doctors that weren't interested in the hospital but liked the location. At the time, there were not many medical buildings being built. It was in a prime location with quick freeway access in an ideal location next to the hospital and, regardless of whether the doctors were actually going to use the hospital facilities, the impression bestowed by the proximity to the hospital gave their practices an additional sense of credibility and prominence. The doctors valued that and it did contribute to their success.

We were able to put one of the top oncologists in Southern California in the building and place one of the few linear accelerators in Southern California in this project. Housing the linear accelerator was a complex project that required the coordination of several contractors and several trades, coordinating both with the specific contractors hired to construct and install the linear accelerator, along with the engineers and physicists that designed the vault in which to place the linear accelerator. The coordination was detailed, complex, and required a great deal of oversight.

In the end, we had 50,000 square feet of medical space occupied by the top dentists and doctors in the state and country. We had a state-of-the-art surgery center, we had one of the top dermatologists in the LA/Orange County area, and most of these doctors *still* operate in the building today. What happened to the doctors that left the building? They sold their practices and/or retired.

Overall, it was a very successful project from both the doctors' perspective as well as ours. We were able to bring a key medical center into the community, providing great value to the doctors and the surrounding area. Ultimately, we were able to sell the building, and using that knowledge, move to the next project.

So, why am I writing this book? First of all, it's critical to the success of your practice. There's no other choice you will make that will more affect the success of your practice, other than perhaps your medical specialty. The amount of money you will spend to properly build out your space and equip it with the tools you'll need to treat your patients is substantial, making you financially committed to that location for a minimum of five years, but usually ten.

Five to ten years in the same location can become problematic. If you enjoy the location, there's no problem at all. However, if the location isn't ideal, you have a problem. In this book, you will learn how to find a location that's right for you. In each chapter you'll learn specific details of the various steps, such as financing, or how to find a good contractor, and how to avoid the many pitfalls that you would otherwise fall into. My goal is to give you the knowledge and confidence you'll need. In essence, you'll know what the developer knows. I don't hold back any information in this book. All the details, all the benefits for the developer, all the benefits for you, the doctor, are discussed. Why? Because I believe by helping you have a successful practice I will be doing my part to help the healthcare industry, particularly entrepreneurial doctors, strengthen and grow. I ultimately want to show doctors that are coming out of school that they can have their own practice and bring value to their family and community. That's my goal in this book.

So, what's the best way to use this book? Well, you could do the traditional cover-to-cover read and that certainly isn't a bad way to go. Only *you* can really decide the best way to use this book. But, there might be a better way than reading cover to cover. Because each step in this process will take several weeks to several months, it would be easy to lose some of the details you've learned about each step. Missing details will get you into trouble. I recommend that you read the chapter that addresses the stage you're at now, whether it be finding a location, locating a broker, negotiating the deal—whatever your situation might be. In essence, I'm suggesting that you use this as a reference book and not as a novel.

I think this approach is going to allow you to get through the process more successfully and retain the details you need as you go. At the end of each chapter, I focus on the things I really want you to remember. After you've read the chapter, it will still be easy for you to revisit it and find the key points you need to review.

As I mentioned, you are the one who's going to need to decide exactly how you can use this book. Whatever choice you make, I am certain this book will help you. I've watched many doctors become very successful, even opening several practices, and it's possible for you to do the same and even enjoy the process. Once you understand a few key principals, you've got the power of knowledge on your side. It's all very easy, really; certainly easier than the things you've already learned in med school, so I encourage you to jump in and use this book in the way that is most profitable to you.

Congratulations on achieving this place in your career, and may God bless your practice.

—Richard T. Boureston
The Boureston Companies
www.tbcos.com

Chapter One
FINDING MEDICAL OFFICE SPACE

Looking for medical or dental office space is really no different than looking for a house. You have several resources available to help you: a *broker*, your friends or family, Internet sites, a mailer you receive, or another doctor. Each avenue has its benefits and detriments and it is important to understand what those are.

Brokers

Otherwise known as real estate agents and generally considered the life-blood of real estate, brokers are traditionally the centerpiece of the transaction. Over the years the brokerage industry has successfully inserted brokers between the seller and buyer.

Typically the seller will sign an exclusive agreement with a broker to represent his property. This agreement gives the broker an assurance that the time and money she spends on marketing the project will not be negated by the owner bypassing the broker and setting up transactions himself. The property owner does not benefit nearly as much from an exclusive agreement except to the extent that nearly all senior real estate brokers require it when they agree to represent the property.

When you are committing $10 million or more to a project, you want to make sure that you have the best team representing you. I always insist on working with the most knowledgeable and skilled broker available when I build a medical office building. In fact, I have been using the same brokerage company for nearly ten years because of the level of trust we have developed. I would encourage you to find a good broker, the best broker you can, if you decide to use a broker to help you find property.

> Much like when Luther translated the Bible into the commoner's language, thereby making the words of the Bible available to the masses, so has the Internet released information once carefully guarded by the few people who controlled it.

But understand that the tools most brokers are using to find property are also available to you on the Internet.

Much like when Luther translated the Bible into the commoner's language, thereby making the words of the Bible available to the masses, so has the Internet released information once carefully guarded by the few people who controlled it. Prior to the Internet, all information was distributed via "fax blasts," something still strongly used by brokers. Fax blasts are simply flyers broadcast-faxed to every broker and brokerage house in the target area. Now, email blasts perform the same task and are faster and more reliable. And that, for the most part, is how brokers advertise a building. It has been effective, but is becoming less so.

While, traditionally, the broker is responsible for marketing and handling the transaction, I have found it better to take more of the marketing into my own hands. This allows the broker to spend more of his time doing what he was trained to do: broker the transaction. The reason brokers are licensed by the State is to ensure their professional ability to guide their client through escrow and assist with the appraisal. Because of the strong need for credibility and professionalism, the State requires that brokers have a basic understanding of several elements of real estate including basic economics. While they may be trained in several aspects of real estate, one thing they are not trained in is how to best market the property and yet that is what the majority of brokers currently do.

Nonetheless, the buyer receives a great deal of information from a good broker, but most of the value a buyer or lessee will find in a senior broker is the explanation of what is standard practice in the real estate industry and what is atypical.

You want to find a broker who is interested in putting a deal together. I have seen too many brokers talk their clients into walking away from opportunities over issues that never should have killed the deal. Ninety-nine percent of the time it happens when a *residential* broker is used. While he or she may be the same card-carrying state-licensed broker as a seasoned commercial broker, they lack the necessary experience to competently and accurately advise you. To be frank, they are in over their head. Commercial real estate is an entirely different ball game on an entirely different field. The only connection is that there is a ball involved. If there is one thing that I have seen readily ruin an otherwise good transaction it is an inexperienced residential broker ill-advising his client.

Commercial brokers traditionally "run" under a senior broker for one year, making nearly no money, while they apprentice and learn their trade. During this time they typically work sixty-hour weeks and in return the senior broker teaches them everything he knows about being a good broker. At the end of the year, the new broker will start getting her own deals and will have learned enough to generally make a six-figure income on her own.

There is no such system established on the residential side, and the lack of knowledge and sophistication shows. You may have a great residential broker, but I cannot recommend enough that you use a commercial broker. The health of your practice depends on it.

If you don't know where to get a good broker, here are a few suggestions.

Look at the Signs

Go to strong medical buildings in the area where you want to run your practice and see what brokerage firm is representing these buildings. Chances are they are senior brokers who have good experience in medical real estate.

Because they are already representing a building, they may try to steer you into that building and not be inclined to show you around. A good broker, however, will look to your interests and recognize that a commission is a commission no matter where it comes from. It should be in his best interest to serve you and meet your needs rather than ram-rod a building down your throat just because he represents that particular building. So my advice is to let the broker know you aren't interested in their building but want them to show you what else is available. They should happily acquiesce.

> ◆
> **You may have a great residential broker, but I cannot recommend enough that you use a commercial broker.**
> ◆

Brokerage Houses

Another excellent way to find a broker is talk to the different brokerage houses in the area. The main brokerage house in an area will have specialists for every type of building use, medical included. Simply ask the receptionist to speak with the brokerage house's office manager, often a seasoned broker who has decided to get out of the game and instead manage other brokers, and explain to the manager you are looking for a senior broker who is experienced in representing doctors looking for medical space. He or she will be happy to point you in the right direction. Because you don't know if there is a political motivation for a certain suggested broker, you still want to ask the broker you end up with a few questions:

- How long have you been a commercial broker?
  (Ten years should be the minimum)
- How many transactions do you average a year?
  (Twenty-five to thirty shows an active broker)
- What experience do you have representing doctors looking for medical space?
- Are you representing any buildings currently?
- Do you have a couple of clients you have worked with on more than one deal that I could talk to about how the transactions went?

The last question may be the most important because you want to know that this person has clients that chose to work with him more than one time. If he cannot point you to at least a couple clients that have used him more than once, then you should probably move on.

Word of Mouth

The most obvious way is to ask other doctors who have done successful transactions in the last year how they liked their broker and if they would recommend him or her. Then ask questions similar to the ones above.

If you focus on finding a good broker, everything else will go smoothly. Ultimately, the broker must be someone you can trust. That "chemistry" will vary depending on your personality and the broker's. Do not think that you should use a broker you do not like just because she is the only one you could find.

Choosing a broker is one situation where you do *not* want to settle. Finding the right broker will mean the difference between contentment and dissatisfaction with your decisions after the transaction is complete. The broker you find must be someone you can put your faith in because inevitably several issues will arise during your negotiations and due diligence.

> **Do not think that you should use a broker you do not like just because she is the only one you could find.**

You will look to your broker to tell you whether what the owner is offering you is in sync with the industry's standard. If you don't trust her, you are going to spend a lot of time double-checking every little statement and you will complete the transaction hoping you never have to do that again.

Online

In the residential industry, a number of online search engines have been available for several years. They have been great assets to both buyers and sellers. Because of the many filters you can apply to your search conditions it is very easy to tell the home search engines exactly what you are looking for.

Unfortunately, when it comes to searching for commercial sites there is not much available to you. The good news is that what is available to you is just as good as the best residential search engine. Even though it really was not on the radar of the Internet even two years ago, Loopnet.com has become the leader in commercial property search engines and really does not have any serious direct competitor that provides the same level of service. Using Loopnet.com, you can search via numerous channels and specifications and be notified when something matches what you are looking for. This allows you to do the same thing as a broker.

Generally speaking, every property that is on the market will be listed on Loopnet.com, so you will not be at a disadvantage when looking for your new space. As a result, Loopnet.com has become another tool every developer expects his broker to use.

You will also find many private sellers listing their property on Loopnet.com.

The benefit: you will know that you will see everything available, and know that no property is being hidden from sight because of a lesser commission or some other reason that might motivate a less-than-professional broker to not show you a property.

Each of the brokerage houses will also have their own database of buildings that they are listing, which you can access via their website. These sites give detailed information about each of the listings and often will have brochures with additional information about the site that can be downloaded. The obvious difficulty with this approach is it requires you to visit every brokerage website you can think of with the hope of finding all the property available.

♦

Choosing a broker is one situation where you do *not* want to settle.

♦

For most doctors, the idea of spending hours looking on various websites is not appealing. I am guessing you are not going to have time. The main reason the brokerage firms put the properties up is to turn over every stone. It really is the hope that people will come to their site, look at their listings, and ultimately close one of their deals. I'm sure this rarely happens but it probably did at one point in the annuals of real estate sales history and so everyone still does it. Your best bet may be finding a medical real estate specialist's website and see what's listed.

Craigslist.org

Craigslist.org is a grassroots classified ads website started in 1995 by Craig Newmark to serve the San Francisco area. Although billed as an 'organization' rather than a 'corporation,' don't be mislead by the '.org' top-level domain, which is typically used by nonprofit organizations. Craigslist.org, although private, is estimated by some to have earned $150 million in the year 2007. With only 25 employees, it now serves 450 cities and 50 countries, as of the last count. It is a strictly text-driven site with little to no graphics and maintains the 1995 design it started with. So it would not typically be a place that a professional would look for office space, nor would a broker typically consider listing a property on it. Yet I do find people listing medical office space on craigslist.org. Everything in selling is about matching the tone and presentation of your communication with the tone and presentation the buyer is looking for. I do believe that someone might enjoy the impression they get from a simple text ad on a humble website. It gives a sense of approachability that is lacking in most medical real estate transactions.

My guess is that the people who are listing on craigslist.org are private owners that have some space available and don't want to pay a commission to a broker. I rarely find anything useful there but as Internet marketing grows, it could be a strong place to advertise. Because it only takes a few minutes to check, I would recommend visiting the site; select your state and city, and then type in "Medical Office" and see if anything comes up. You just might get lucky.

Newspaper Classifieds

All newspapers have online classifieds that list everything similar to what you would find on Craigslist.org. I have personally seen their usefulness decrease steadily over the last several years as more and more of the real estate world transfers to online media using specialized websites like Loopnet.com to "get the word out." It is probably not going to be productive and is really no different than visiting every brokerage house's site, except that there is typically only one or two large newspapers in an area so there will be fewer to review. Of course, this decision is a matter of how much time you have; you may want to delegate the job to another person who can do the grunt work for you.

Mailers

You probably get several of these mailers a day if you already have a practice or are part of a group. Depending on your instructions to your front office you may or may not even see them. The mailers themselves now typically come in the form of a postcard-sized advertisement that often has a picture and a map and some details about the building or site on both sides. Often glossy, they tend to all look the same. If real estate isn't on your mind (which is doubtful since you are reading this book), you might be inclined to throw the mailers away. But that would be unwise.

> If real estate isn't on your mind (which is doubtful since you are reading this book), you might be inclined to throw the mailers away. But that would be unwise.

There are some very helpful pieces of information on each of those mailers, but they don't become helpful unless you have several of them. Every mailer will contain the building information, which includes the square feet available in the building as well as the location. It becomes very easy, over time, to get a real sense of an area's competitive nature by collecting and noting how many medical buildings are in the area and the square feet available. If you don't have a broker, the mailer is also an excellent way to find successful brokers in the area. When you start noticing that the same broker is representing several important medical buildings in the area, you have just saved yourself a lot of time and can now put her on your list of brokers to interview when you decide to start seriously looking.

The simplest way to handle the mailers is to ask your front office to file them as they arrive so you can review them at your leisure.

Where Do You Look?

While the three most important things in real estate are "Location, Location, Location," unfortunately that tired saying doesn't tell you *which* location to pick. You might be inclined to say, "I'm picking the location that generates the most money," but if that means you have to move across the country, that may or may not be your best choice. There are actually several "best" locations you can choose from and all of them are incredibly valid choices, it just depends on your criteria.

Near the House

Probably the biggest reason I've heard for why someone chose a practice location was because it was in close proximity to his or her house. As one doctor put it, "We drew the circle and that's the area we were looking for." Obviously, quality of life is an important consideration when you are looking for space. If you consider that you will most likely be driving to the same place for ten years, then you truly can test the validity of one location over another strictly by the commute each requires. Knowing that you will invest likely $80,000–$200,000 of your own money on tenant improvements (the interior build out), nearly $500,000 if you are a dentist, should cause you to pause and realize you are not going anywhere for a long time. I'm hoping you live in a thriving area where many patients need your services and there is a low patient/doctor ratio. Otherwise, you may want to consider moving or be comfortable with the idea of a longer commute than you may have originally desired.

> If you consider that you will most likely be driving to the same place for ten years, then you truly can test the validity of one location over another strictly by the commute each requires.

Near a Hospital

I don't think it is necessary for me to explain why you may want to be near a hospital. The fact is that you either care that you are near a hospital or you don't. If you don't have patients that will need to use the services available in the hospital, it probably doesn't help you to pay what is often higher rent to be in close proximity to the hospital. On the other hand, if your services are closely tied to the hospital and they are seeking your skills, you can expect the hospital to provide you with below-market rent and strong patient referrals, the latter of which will help you build your practice quickly.

Often the hospital will Master Lease a portion of an adjacent medical office building and then place the services they need into that space. The hospital's signature is on the lease, which makes the developer happy. More importantly, your signature is *not*, which should make you happy. So if something happens, you are not going to have to deal with the developer because the hospital will continue to pay rent even though you may have decided to end your relationship with the hospital. Typically, the financial commitments from the hospital for your practice will require commitments on your part, most often in the form of loans that are forgiven if you complete your contracted term. At the end of your contractual commitment, you will be free to do what you want. You will be able to walk away and find a bigger, better, and more lucrative place to operate, if you so desire.

The truth is that your location next to the hospital is probably a fantastic place to operate, and will most likely be the place you will want to remain. In this case, you might consider opening a second location, and this location will probably require a contribution on your part. Your experience in the first location will give you a significant head start on your second and it is not uncommon for the second location to become profitable much more quickly than the first. And the nice part of the story is that you "cut your teeth on" on the hospital's nickel, not yours.

Key Intersections

One of the most common factors that a *retail* business looks at is the amount of traffic that drives by the site. Most of their business comes from people driving by and seeing their sign from the street. Whether this should be important to you is something you ultimately will have to decide, but I believe there are a few things I can help you with in this area.

For the true retailer, they not only want to have a lot of cars driving by, such as the volume a freeway brings, but they also particularly want cars in front of their sign for the longest period of time possible. This is why a major national coffee company (I'll let you fill in the gaps) focuses mostly on signalized intersections. If the cars are forced to stop, the drivers will have more time to look around.

———— ◆ ————
Without a sign, you are not really benefiting from the dense drive-by traffic.
———— ◆ ————

Without a sign, you are not really benefiting from the dense drive-by traffic. Because of the pace of traffic these days drivers do not have time to look out their window and try to figure what your store offers them. You have to tell them and you have to tell them in .002 seconds, unless of course there is a signal at the intersection. A signal will force them to stop at that intersection for at least two minutes and your impression time just increased exponentially.

Underserved Area

One common reason I hear doctors cite for choosing a location is that they have found there is a low ratio of their specialty to people. This can be compelling to someone who doesn't have a patient base and wants to start building in a low competitive area. It also will require a minimum of a two-year commitment for someone who has no marketing infrastructure in place. I have seen practices become profitable in less time, but only when the doctors had previously opened and operated a practice.

Keep in mind that if the government agrees it is an underserved area, there are grants available to help you establish your practice to serve that community.

Types of Building Uses

Parking

In all cities, parking is the way the planning department controls what type of use can function on any particular piece of land. Generally it is quoted as a number of parking spots per thousand square feet of building, although I have seen it quoted at 'per 250' square feet of building. The reason 'per thousand' matters is that it is easy to divide into the number of square feet of gross building square footage. For instance, most medical use is required to "park" the building at 5 parking stalls per 1,000 gross building square feet. If you have a building that is 40,000 square feet, you will be required to provide 200 parking stalls to meet the requirement.

You are not a developer, so why do you care about this? Because it directly affects the price of the building. If I pay $20 per square foot of land and the land is 1 acre in size, then the land will cost me $871,200 (43,560 square feet x $20). I have to capitalize on that expense as much as possible, and in most places the tenant won't accept being charged for parking. There are, of course, downtown metropolitan areas that do charge parking to their tenants, but most suburban areas don't. Because it is essential that I get as much building on the land as possible, I'm usually happy if I can get 30 percent coverage in a suburban area; it can be much greater coverage in a downtown location. Remember, this is all driven by the parking requirements, so if the land is 43,560 square feet, I can put 13,068 gross square feet of building on that site. I make my money on 13,068 square feet even though I had to buy the 43,560 square feet and then probably spend another $5 per square foot of land for site work such as curbs, gutters, pavement, and grading. So before I even build the building the project is costing me $83.33 per square foot of building, $871,200 (land cost) + $217,800 (site work cost) then divide by 13,068 square feet. And that is just looking at those few costs, not all the soft costs like engineering and architectural, attorney fees, and city plan check and permits.

The point is that if I could put a 30,000 gross square foot building on that site, it would only cost me $36.30 per square foot of building instead of $83.33. You can see how the parking ratio is an enormous contribution to the end cost you will pay in the form of rent or purchase price. Simplistically speaking, if all other things are equal, I could lower my price by $47 a foot and still make the same amount of money. It is important that the building be "parked" enough to support the number of patients using the building. Nonetheless, traffic studies show that most fully occupied buildings use roughly three parking spots per thousand, not five. Think how much cheaper that could be for you!

In fact, parking requirements are why medical and retail has higher rent than professional office or industrial. It is also why most medical use is allowed within retail buildings; the parking ratio is often the same, or higher.

──────── ◆ ────────
It is very important that you have products that can increase your base fees because it is incredibly expensive to get your patient into your practice; once they are there, it becomes critical that you maximize the time available with this patient.
──────── ◆ ────────

Retail

There are certain types of doctors who do well in retail centers. Instead of listing them I will simply point out their similar attributes.

They are a retail-like operation.

These types of practices have the number one ability necessary to perform well in a retail environment: up-sell. It is very important that you have products that can increase your base fees because it is incredibly expensive to get your patient into your practice; once they are there, it becomes critical that you maximize the time available with this patient. There will be an important balance that occurs between maintaining credibility and increasing profit, but make no mistake, increasing profit must be your goal because you are paying top dollar for every square foot of your space.

So your business must naturally allow for the type of conversation where you will be able to suggest services or products without sounding like a coat-wearing watch vendor. It will become obvious that a proctologist does not lend itself naturally to an up-selling type of conversation.

On the other hand, general dentists and urgent care clinics can flourish in these types of environments, and you will find that the more general your practice, the more naturally it will fit into the retail environment.

Even though the price will often be prohibitive, it has been communicated to me by other doctors that the perception of credibility and expertise often lessens if they are located in a retail center. If you decide to be in a retail center, understand that people will view your practice differ-

> **If you decide to be in a retail center, understand that people will view your practice differently than if you were in a medical building.**

ently than if you were in a medical building. Your patient will view your practice from a more retail perspective and expect a retail-type service and will most likely not feel the same type of loyalty to you that they would feel if you were in a medical building.

Medical

Medical office buildings are the obvious choice for most doctors, and I have been told that dental doctors like the professional atmosphere of a medical building as well. Even before I was told this I understood that dentists liked to be in my medical projects because they would often occupy half of the building. I have to agree that there is an important distinction between retail and medical and if you haven't guessed, I'm partial to medical. Because I run a professional company I am sensitive to the perception others hold of our company. It is important that my office, my staff, my consultants, and I make those that interact with my company feel that they are dealing with professionalism on every level. I know that there is a deep amount of trust that needs to exist between my company and the tenants or buyers that move into our buildings and use our services.

It is equally important that you present yourself in such a way that your patients are instilled with overwhelming confidence about your level of commitment to them and their health. They want to know that you are more concerned about their health than your bottom line. It is my belief you will be most successful by having your practice in the most professional-looking building possible.

Dental

Dental use is also considered medical use, from the government's perspective. The difference in dental use comes with the design and construction, and we will discuss more of that in chapter 4 when we talk about space planning and chapter 5 where we talk about construction. Because of the requirements of dental equipment, it will be important to find a building constructed within the last few years as it will most likely have the electrical system necessary to support the draw your new equipment will require.

Professional Office

The only case where your practice would work in a professional office situation is if the owner "over-parked" the building—that is, he created more parking spaces than are required for the intended use. I have built office buildings where I built enough parking such that I could fill 25 percent of my building with medical type use and the remaining 75 percent with professional office. This allows me to market to both types of tenants, thereby putting my eggs in more than one basket. In most areas it is unusual for doctors to choose a professional office building to run their practice, but there are some places I have built where it is common. You will need to consider the area you are in and see what is generally accepted and check that against what your gut tells you about your patients, or the patients you hope to get.

Ultimately, you need to know your patient base, the type of building you are considering, and how that will affect the perception your patients will have of your practice.

New or Old Building

Deciding whether to use a new or old building usually comes down to cost and location, although at some point in an area's existence you will not have a choice between the two. Even in areas like Orange County or Los Angeles, California, however, there are still new buildings under construction. Often, in places like Los Angeles, the price a developer can receive for a medical use building is high enough that he can justify knocking an existing building down and putting up a new building. In Orange County, we are seeing a resurgence of new medical buildings replacing old industrial or office buildings. This can be a great benefit for you if you desire to be in a location that has no medical buildings. When you have a new building, you can decide exactly how your space is going to be laid out, the finishes you will use, and the amount of space you need.

With the ability to make decisions about your design and construction comes the financial commitment necessary to contribute toward their related expenses. Typically, the landlord will contribute a certain number of dollars per useable square feet; we'll discuss how that differs from rentable square feet in chapter 2. While there is no point in telling you how much your suite will cost, you should currently plan on contributing at least $80,000 and up to $500,000 toward the design and construction of the suite, assuming a standard size suite of about 2,000 square feet. Fortunately, the bank will factor that into your business loan, and you will not have to come up with the money in cash. It will, however, be a significant monthly cost and something you will have to plan for while executing your feasibility study.

In a new building, the common area will be new and up to date with current colors and designs and your patients will sense they are in a new place that is exciting. Obviously, the building will reflect the most current adjustments in codes for all trades, and you can be assured that all the new American Disability Act (ADA) requirements are met. Additionally, the electrical, mechanical, and plumbing will all be designed with the latest information available to the engineers and include the most current equipment, which will significantly lower utility expenses.

While that may be compelling, there is often the simple need to minimize costs, and an existing space can be the best way to accomplish that goal. Because you will move into a suite where the tenant improvements have already been completed, you do not have to wait the typical five to eight months it takes to design and construct your suite. In addition, you won't have to stop what you are doing for months while you review and decide upon a million decisions—from finishes to where to place the electrical outlets, to the width of the corridors and depth of the patient rooms. Most of that will be decided for you by the previous tenant, and you will simply need to adjust the color of wall paint and type of carpet or flooring. This makes it a much simpler process and can be an excellent choice for someone who is extremely busy. Many doctors have told me they underestimated the amount of time it took them to get through the whole process, and how it directly affected their existing practice or work. It has often been said to me, "If I'm not in the office seeing patients, then I'm not making money." If all your time is consumed by design layouts and carpet colors, your income will most certainly be negatively affected.

> **Many doctors have told me they underestimated the amount of time it took them to get through the whole process, and how it directly affected their existing practice or work.**

There are also times when you need a space quickly. This most often happens when you haven't planned ahead and suddenly realized your existing lease is ending in three months and you haven't started looking for a new location. An existing suite will be the only option you have, unless you have an understanding landlord who is willing to allow you to "holdover" your lease beyond the contracted term. Often when this happens you should expect to pay 150 percent of your original rent. The point isn't to gouge you, but rather to motivate you not to stay longer than you absolutely must.

Existing space is also an excellent choice when it comes to finances. You will not have to lay out tens of thousands of dollars, which may not even be possible, and you will not be as financially committed to the building as you will be when you build out your own suite. This is great news if you just need a launching pad to embed yourself in the community and know that once you become profitable and established, you will move to a more prestigious location where you can take the lessons you have learned from this location and make the necessary corrections.

As with all things, it is not all sugar and spice when it comes to existing buildings. Because they were built before the new codes were implemented, they may not be up to current standards and you should ensure they comply with ADA guidelines. More importantly, the equipment has most likely passed its warranty period, most often a year for all mechanical equipment and elevator equipment, so it will become more of a burden on the owner to maintain the property. Some landlords take pride in their buildings and properly maintain them despite the cost. Others refuse to do anything to the building. It is in your best interest to make sure you do not move into a building where your landlord is non-responsive to your maintenance requests. I would recommend you have discussions with several doctors in the building and verify any information you might be told by the landlord. If the tenants inform you that the landlord does nothing and your inspectors verify this information, then you should probably keep looking. I know it isn't common to hire an inspector to review the building when you are leasing, but it is an excellent way to know what you are getting yourself into before you sign a five- or ten-year commitment.

> **As with all things, it is not all sugar and spice when it comes to existing buildings.**

Type of Construction

While most doctors won't think twice about how a building was constructed, there are some elements of construction that can affect your office design options and how your finished product meets your expectations. Most often, construction choices are based on the current market's requirement for design and the cost of materials at the time of construction. The materials used to construct a building can vary greatly from building to building within the same area. While some professionals in the real estate industry will view certain materials as inferior, and I am not going to bore you with presenting each side of the argument, I do feel it is necessary to explain why you should care and what, specifically, you should care about.

The primary focus for you should be whether the building is well sound-insulated and, most importantly, waterproof. Because of today's governmental standards, most buildings built in the past ten years and or later are sufficient at resisting most of what nature can throw at them. Whether the building is made of concrete, block, wood, or steel, it has met the requirements of the local or state government.

From this point I would suggest it is more relevant whether the building is aesthetically pleasing or has the amenities that are important to you. If you want an all-glass building, steel will be your choice as it will allow for the greatest amount of glass at the most reasonable price. But, whether the building is made of steel, block, or wood, you should not be dissuaded from choosing that building. All of these materials are able to attenuate sound and keep water from entering the building. Some materials require additional help from insulation or exterior systems to accomplish sound attenuation or a waterproof status. But at the end of the day you will still get the same result.

> **The primary focus for you should be whether the building is well sound-insulated and, most importantly, waterproof.**

While the exterior of the building will typically not have any functional effect on your practice, the floor and roofing system will greatly affect how content you will be in your new space.

Flooring Systems

There are several ways to get a finished floor on the second and following levels of a building. What is important for you to understand is how the two main ways that flooring systems are built can affect you. A structural engineer will typically design the flooring system based on whether the developer wants a metal deck or plywood deck. So, let's focus on how a metal deck or plywood deck can affect your practice.

If you are below a plywood deck, you will have more risk of hearing noise from the floor above. If you are standing on a plywood deck, you will have more risk of feeling a bounce as you step. The plywood deck is common in residential buildings. There are ways to design a flooring system that addresses these issues and we have done so successfully in the past, but these are the typical traits you will find in a wood deck system.

If you are below a metal composite deck, you will *not* hear noise from above. If you are standing on a metal composite deck, you will *not* feel any bounce. A metal composite deck is made of structural concrete poured over a metal deck. The concrete bonds and becomes part of the metal deck; this allows the flooring system to support a much greater load.

Too frequently, doctors will place loads on the floors that the flooring system was never designed to support. Normally, this won't show up in everyday use, but if nature applies additional forces to the building, these overloaded areas are the places that structural failings show up first. Keep this information in mind as you investigate different buildings.

Whether the deck is metal or wood, there is a simple but effective way to figure out if the flooring system will work for you: have the person you are with go upstairs and walk around and jump up and down as you stand below and listen. Do you hear any noise? Did the jumper feel any bounce? If the space you are standing in has not been completed, you will be able to *see* if it is a metal deck or plywood deck. If you are intent on the moving into building and are unsure of the flooring system, then request a set of plans and ask your contractor or architect to walk you through them and explain to you how the building was constructed.

Roofing Materials

The roof will most likely be constructed similarly to the floor. The difference is how the roof is completed. Unlike a floor, which is designed for people to stand on, the roof is designed to support equipment and protect the interior from the elements. A slope in the roof is one of the best ways to guarantee the protection of the interior and will be easy for you to note.

Stationary water has the best opportunity to work its way into the building. Keeping water moving toward the roof drains gives the roof the best chance to control the water and keep it from getting through the waterproof membrane.

There are three common ways to do this: three-ply, four-ply, and single-ply.

The number of plies on a roof denotes the number of layers of roofing material that are laid on the roof system. Therefore, three-ply indicates three layers of roofing material were applied to the roof system, and so on. Generally, the only reason you would use three-ply is to save money; four-ply provides much better protection. The main weakness with this design is that every joint gives the water an opportunity to break through the waterproof membrane. On the average four-ply roof, there are hundreds to thousands of joints. This is true for the three-ply design as well.

On the other hand, a single-ply is a thicker layer that is as close to seamless as possible. There are very few joints and the joints that do exist are welded to provide the greatest assurance of protection. While the roofing sub-contractor will normally provide a five-year warranty for a four-ply roof, I just recently used a single-ply roof and the roofing sub-contractor gave me a ten-year warranty at the same cost as the four-ply system. The single-ply system is really that much better.

A well-constructed roof and floor will ensure you can run a practice that won't be disturbed by noise or weather. While it is not typically a factor for most doctors I have talked with, the construction of the building *should* play a role in your decision.

THINGS *to* REMEMBER

1. Use a commercial broker, no matter what a residential broker may tell you.

2. Use websites like Loopnet.com.

3. Keep in mind whom you are targeting when you choose your location.

4. Pay attention to the important elements of construction, particularly the flooring system and roofing system.

Chapter Two
NEGOTIATING THE DEAL

―――― **Get Past the Person and Focus on the Problem** ――――

When my second child was five years old she was terrified of being called a big girl. We would tell her how big she was getting or how her clothes didn't fit her and that she was growing up, typical things parents say to their child. And every time we did she would burst out crying and insist she was not a big girl and was not growing up. This went on for a couple of months and while we didn't think much of it, we were curious why it mattered so much to her but we never asked her why. Because she is more sensitive than our other children, we wrote it off as another example of her sensitive nature.

It wasn't until several months went by that my wife finally asked her why she was so upset about being a "big girl," and that's when I got the call at my office.

"You're not going to believe this."

"Did someone get hurt?"

"No, I found out why Elyse doesn't like us calling her 'big girl.'"

"Really?!? So what's the reason?"

"You know she is terrified of Splash Mountain at Disneyland, right?"

"Sure."

"Well she is afraid that if she gets big then she will be tall enough to go on the ride."

"You've got to be kidding! That's why?"

And so the code was cracked and we finally understood why fear struck the heart of Elyse every time we told her how big she was getting.

This was a silly example of how a person's behavior may obscure the real problem. Of course she wasn't upset about being a big girl—she was upset that being a big girl meant she would have to go on the roller coaster ride, and *that* was the problem!

Don't assume that what a person says or does is the reason they are saying or doing it. There may be a very different reason, and it is your job to get to the bottom of it. Focus on the *problem*; the person is immaterial. Once we understood the real problem for Elyse, we were able to comfort her and let her know that she did not have to go on the amusement park ride until she wanted. The crying stopped immediately, and she never cried about growing up again. We got past the posturing and the dramatics, and finally got to the problem.

> ♦
> **Don't assume that what a person says or does is the reason they are saying or doing it.**
> ♦

You have to get past the problem if you want to be successful. And by successful I mean: get a financially viable deal *and* establish a strong relationship with the other party. Rarely in life are there transactions that occur where you will never interact with that person again. There are relationships that I built up years ago that didn't directly affect me in a positive way until many years later. Likewise, there are relationships I burned that, years later, directly affected my business.

Discuss each other's perceptions of the situation, and be open to the idea that there may be an excellent reason for this person's otherwise ridiculous behavior or request. If you can discover the underlying reason, you are very far down the path to a successful solution.

Your perceptions and your interests are important—to you. Make the other person's perceptions equally important. You can begin by clearly communicating how you see things and why you see them that way. However, if you stop there, you are wasting your time. Give the other side an opportunity to share their thoughts. If what they are saying doesn't seem credible or logical, find out why.

It is possible that what you think you hear them saying is not what they are trying to say, no matter how obvious it may appear. The only way to know for sure is to ask, "It seems that when the rent starts is very important to you. Is that true?" Based on the answer, you can then start working together to build a solution. By doing this you are including the other party in the solution process. It is far better to have them participate in designing a solution than having a solution presented to them with no ownership on their part. With ownership comes the perception of value because they are now invested in the product.

> **Your perceptions and your interests are important—to you. Make the other person's perceptions equally important.**

I was in a situation once where we had tried several times to have a tenant take some additional space in our building. It seemed like the perfect choice for her and yet we could not get her to commit. We finally learned that while she had been giving us all kinds of other reasons, it was really the fact that she needed to get out of her lease that was keeping her from expanding. She was leasing from a doctor who had purchased some space from me in the same building. Once I found out the real reasons and confirmed that her current lease was the only issue keeping her from signing a lease with me, I had the information I needed to put a deal together and the commitment from her that she would sign a lease with me if I was able to terminate her current lease.

Emotions

Controlling your emotions and at the same time not letting the emotions of others derail your progress is essential to a successful negotiation. It is critical that you focus intensely on resolving the outstanding issues and not be distracted by extraneous antics and events irrelevant to the solution. When blustering and caustic words are spoken, remaining focused can be difficult. I can assure you, however, if you get caught up in the whirlwind, you will lose control of your direction and will not end up where you intended. Instead of avoiding the emotions, acknowledge them, talk about them, describe them, and then they will lose their power over you and others. By talking about your feelings you give the other party an opportunity to feel free to share their feelings.

> **The goal of keeping your cool and listening is not to feel better as a person, but rather to get the real reason and then move on.**

I recently received a call from a doctor who was upset at our company for lack of communication. I had never spoken to her before, but heard she was difficult to talk with. As she initiated the conversation by trying to put me in my place and talking to me as though I was three years old, I patiently listened until she finished. I then answered each of her comments in a calm voice and asked several more questions that brought clarity to the situation. By the end of the conversation she informed me that she wished she had spoken to me in the first place and shortly after signed an agreement to purchase some space from me.

The goal of keeping your cool and listening is not to feel better as a person, but rather to get the real reason and then move on. Be disciplined in pursuing the underlying reasoning behind the emotion and you will be rewarded. Often, a person can be very emotionally tied to the outcome of a negotiation and he will feel very anxious toward any suggestions or statements you may make, which lead him to believe you are not going to give him what he wants. If you can find out what happens if he doesn't get his way, then you will have an opportunity to give him his way in a manner that directly benefits you.

Bottom line, if you work to move in the same direction as the other party, most of the difficulties will end. There are some key strategies to accomplishing this: focus on interests, not positions; use community problem solving; and use objective data to establish a reference point.

Interests Not Positions

Positions are what we want. Interests are why we want it. When a child declares that she is not tired, she is taking a position in opposition to the mother who thinks the child is tired. The child's position is she wants to stay up. The mother's position is she wants the child to sleep. In this obvious situation it is clear that it is not sleep the child is against, but rather it's the request from her mother to stop what she is doing that is the problem.

The same is true for real estate negotiations. I just recently met with some doctors that had negotiated with me for three weeks; we had come to an agreement, and my attorney had drawn the purchase agreement for them to sign. Usually at this point everything is done and 99 percent of the time the documents are signed and everything proceeds ahead. This wasn't the situation, and after three weeks of talking back and forth about a particular issue and thinking it was resolved, I finally realized this wasn't going to be resolved until I met with the doctors. I knew what the issue was and was prepared to discuss it. They wanted a warranty on the building since they would be the first ones in it. Normally, this wouldn't be a problem, but the building was in a difficult market and had remained empty for a year after construction was completed. I no longer had any warranty on the building from my contractor, and I was not interested in providing something that wasn't provided to me. So we had our stand-off: warranty or no warranty.

After meeting with them and discussing the matter, they came to learn that I wasn't trying to hide something, which they had originally assumed, but rather that they were asking something from me that I didn't have to give them.

I learned that they were concerned that something might happen to the plumbing or air conditioning after they moved in and they would be stuck with the bill. The solution we agreed to was that I would make sure there was an adequate reserve available in the association account (this was a medical condominium project) to cover any typical problems that might arise in the first year. After three weeks of wrangling, it only took one hour of talking at a meeting and the papers were signed. Because putting some money into the reserve wasn't an issue for me, and being liable for anything that could possibly happen to the building wasn't acceptable to me, and because the doctors didn't care about the warranty as much as what the warranty represented (protection from unforeseen financial burdens), we were able to strike a deal that was mutually beneficial.

While it may seem common sense that each person has his or her own interests, it is not always easy to discern what they are, especially when they are purposely being kept from you. Asking "Why . . . ?" can provide the answer to your problem. Most often the answer will fall into one of the following categories:

1. Control
2. Security
3. Recognition

Control can be in the form of control over one's financial situation, or control over one's future. The bottom line is it can take the form of many reasons, but by asking, "Why do you want this?" it might become evident. Maybe the lessee wants control over the rent for the next ten years and is insisting on a ten-year lease rather than a five-year lease (maybe the location or features of the building are so phenomenal that he knows he will not be leaving for at least ten years). It could also be as simple as he wants to be able to amortize tenant improvement costs over the ten-year period. If more than one answer could be the reason, it is all right to ask, "I understand you want a ten-year lease, but most people are happy *not* being committed to such a long-term agreement. Can you explain to me why a ten-year term is so important to you?"

Security is another basic human need that can be unnoticed if you focus only on positions. A $10,000 security deposit may seem like a lot for a landlord to ask, but when you understand that it brings security to the landlord by knowing that he now has a strong and committed tenant, it becomes easier to understand. It is usually possible to negotiate some of these security issues; after a year of no blemishes, for example, the landlord can return the security deposit to the tenant knowing that the tenant is now operating and functioning well in the building.

Recognition is one of the biggest inciters of turmoil. I have seen many deals get blown over the need for respect, a word often used interchangeably with the word "recognition." The other party wants to know that you value what they bring to the table and that you recognize they are not a "dime a dozen" but an important relationship you want to foster and develop. If you get a strong emotional reaction to an offer you make, it would be wise to consider how you may have disrespected the other party or otherwise not recognized their value.

> **Recognition is one of the biggest inciters of turmoil.**

This is especially true when you work with the Chinese. Their culture teaches them a long-term view of relationships. They understand that very few relationships are short term. Additionally, their shame-based culture will cause them to see your actions from a perspective not shared in the Western world. At the same time, a strong emotional reaction can be used as a tactic to force you to acquiesce to their position. By asking questions about the source of their reaction, you will be able to quickly discern whether it is a sincere response or a tactic. Regardless of the answer, you are not obligated to weaken your position based on their perception or response.

The important element to remember while going through this process is this: the point is not to learn everything you can about the other side so you can give away everything important to you. You need to understand what is important to the other side in relation to what is important to you as part of your negotiating strength. By doing this, you will have the greatest possibility of reaching a solution that benefits both parties.

Brainstorming

Here is where the rubber meets the road. You have done all this work to learn about the interests of the other party, and you have taken the time to understand your own interests. You should now have all the information you need to develop some options that consider everyone's interests and concerns. Dig deep; the solution might not be obvious, but with the right preparation you should discover the right answer.

When I first got out of school I moonlighted as a programmer for a couple years. One guideline we developed that proved very useful was that when we had a problem for which the solution wasn't obvious, we wouldn't stop thinking about it until we came up with three distinct solutions. I encourage you to do the same. It would be unfortunate for you to miss an important opportunity for your practice because you didn't take the time to find the right solution.

Of course, there will be times when you will realize there is no option available to solve the problem and you will have to walk away from the deal. Know that this is not as common as one might think. Yes, it happens every day, but it is my belief that it doesn't need to happen as frequently as it does. If the landlord needs $5 a square foot for rent because he paid $200 a square foot for the land, but you can only afford $2 a square foot (and that is seriously stretching your budget), you might have to go your separate ways if neither of you can find a way to bring additional value to the table. Nonetheless, it is worth spending the time to think about it because you will spend more time starting over with a new location and a new building owner.

Use Objective Data

As I mentioned before, one of the great elements a seasoned and senior broker brings to the process is an ability to settle a tenant's anxiety by assuring them what the landlord is proposing is *standard within the industry*. One of the other resources available through brokers is comparable property reports. These reports will tell you the square footage available in comparable buildings, and the rent or purchase price being asked. This can be an excellent resource that helps you understand the market. You may find that the landlord you are dealing with is asking far more than is reasonable in the area and has no reasonable justification. On the other hand, you may find that what you originally thought was a horrible deal is actually a great deal, now that you have seen what else is available out there. There are standards in every industry—from contractors to attorneys to architects—and each expert can shed light on a particular question or situation.

Documents can be another source of authority. The American Industrial Real Estate Association (AIR) form is an industry agreed-upon form that contains standard language that has been case-tested and found to be both practical and defendable in court. It was generated originally by brokers in 1960 and has continued to be an accepted standard form in the commercial real estate industry. The language is frequently updated to reflect current trends and court case interpretations.

We have often used this document when we entering a basic transaction that does not require much adjustment to what is "normal." Because the AIR form is a standard form, however, the program does not allow you to delete irrelevant sections or language of the lease that isn't pertinent to your transaction. Instead, you are only allowed to "strike through" language and this has been a source of confusion on many deals. More than one doctor has asked me why I don't want to give them the three-year warranty, why I crossed that out. I then spend several conversations explaining to them that we never had a three-year warranty; that it is boilerplate language that doesn't apply to the discussed project. I can only give them a one-year warranty because my contractor can only give me a one-year warranty, I explain. In a sense, it would be like asking the car dealer to give you a ten-year warranty when the manufacturer is only providing the dealer a five-year warranty. If we had been able to delete the language all together, then we could have saved both parties much time. So, be aware that while the AIR is very useful in certain situations, it also is a source of confusion when not viewed in an appropriate light.

> **The point is not to learn everything you can about the other side so you can give away everything important to you.**

Whatever source you decide to use—a broker or form or industry report—the point is to establish a third-party base on which both parties can stand. You need to feel secure and have a reason for your position. "Splitting the difference," as I see so many Westerners do, is looked down upon by certain cultures and you will lose the other party's respect. Have a good reason why you want what you want. And what you want is to be able to point at a chart and say, "Ten other buildings in the area are offering the same rent." That is a much stronger place to start than to say, "My brother got his rent for half of what you are asking."

Common Terms

Here are some important concepts you will come across as you start looking for space, negotiating the deal, and looking at the lease or purchase agreement.

i. Useable Square Feet versus Rentable Square Feet

The difference between useable and rentable square footage is the most common question I get from both brokers and doctors. Useable square footage is the physical space you will be occupying in the building. This often includes half of the walls and can be measured in many different ways based on many different methods or standards. Building Owners and Managers Association (BOMA) can be used, but is typically only relevant in high-rise buildings; if you are moving into a two- or three-story building, BOMA generally will not be a valid way of measuring the space. Because of the vast differences in the market, it is imprudent for me to discuss all the different measuring methods. It is important to note that it can be an arbitrary method decided upon by the developer. So long as the developer uses the same method for all the occupants, it will not put you at a disadvantage. If he changes the method of measuring with each tenant, not only will he have a physical problem in the building (because he will end up with either dead space or overlapping space), but he will also have a problem with the doctors who will most likely deem the act as an injustice.

Rentable square footage includes what is called a "load factor." The load factor considers the amount of space the common area is comprised of in the building, and while the load factor typically excludes vertical shafts like elevators and HVAC ducts, even these exclusions will vary based on the local market. For instance, if the entire building is 30,000 square feet and the common area consumes 10,000 square feet, then the load factor is 33 percent. That means that if your useable square feet is 3,000 feet, then your rentable square feet will be a result of multiplying 1.33 (load factor) x 3000 (useable square feet) equaling 3,990 square feet.

You are charged a load factor because it cost the developer money to build the lobby and corridors and public bathrooms your patients and you will use as you function in the building. It is all provided as a benefit to you, and so the developer should be compensated for that expense. If the developer were to build a retail or R&D-type

building that consisted of outside corridors and no bathrooms or lobby, that would significantly reduce your load factor. It would also significantly reduce the professional image of the building.

While I used an example of 33 percent, typically I see medical buildings with a load factor of 14 percent to 17 percent. I have learned that load factors are generally a sore spot for most doctors, and the bigger the load the deeper the soreness, so over the years I have found the smaller the load factor the less complaints I receive. Look for a building with a low load factor, anything under 20 percent, you'll find it won't affect your bottom line enough to lose the deal.

ii. Common area

Common area is the area inside and outside the building. Another, and perhaps easier, way of looking at it is: the common area is everything outside of your suite. That includes the other half of the walls, unless there is a tenant space on the other side, between the floors, the corridors, lobby, common area bathrooms, mailroom, electric room, elevator equipment room, including the outside seating areas and walkways. While the common area is an element in the load factor calculation, outside areas are typically not included unless there is a compelling reason.

Leases

There are three basic types of leases used in commercial real estate: triple net lease, modified gross lease, and gross lease. In reality there are infinite variations on these types of leases, but these are the ones you will most often find on the market. I have found the easiest way to remember what each does is to keep in mind that the one thing that doesn't change is the amount of money you are paying to physically occupy the space of your practice. If you have agreed to pay two dollars per square foot for your space, then that agreement remains in place typically from month to month, but it usually changes at each anniversary. What makes a lease a triple-net, modified gross, or gross is how the costs related to operating the building are allocated between the owner and you.

What is included in the cost of operating a building? The short answer is: many things. The real answer is: it depends on the specific needs of the building at any given time. While security is not normally needed for a suburban multi-tenant building in a good neighborhood, if an issue arises, a security guard may be brought in for several months to protect the area. On the other hand, security is always included in a high-rise building.

Here are the usual expenses you will have for a commercial medical building: cleaning, repairs and maintenance, elevator, heating and air conditioning, electrical, structural and roofing, plumbing, fire and life safety, general building interior, general building exterior, common area utilities, tenant electrical, tenant janitorial, tenant water, tenant gas, roads and grounds, landscaping, garage, security, administrative, parking operations, taxes, and insurance. Of course, if there is no elevator, you will not see that expense, but this is a good list and covers 98 percent of what you should expect to pay for, in some amount.

I do feel obligated to mention that you pay for most of this whether or not it is broken out as a separate expense. These are real costs, and if the developer has to absorb some or all of them, you should expect to pay higher rent than if you absorb all of them.

Triple Net Lease

A triple net lease is a lease where the tenant is responsible for every cost related to the maintenance and operation of the building. This includes property tax and utilities for both you, as well as what the building common area uses. It will often include the property management fee, which covers the expense of a professional property manager, whether in-house or contracted by the developer. The fees you are charged are referred to as a common area maintenance fee

(CAM) and they include landscape maintenance, janitorial services, window washing, common area electrical usage, and water fees, as well as many other services all covered under and paid for by the CAM fees. They are important because they ensure that the building will continue to look as professional and maintained as the day you decided to start your practice there.

Modified Gross Lease

A modified gross lease sits squarely between a triple net lease and a full gross lease. In a modified gross lease, the property manager generates an estimate that considers the expenses related to the project. He then will break the total costs out on a per square foot basis. That estimate becomes the "base" and will be paid by the landlord for either some or all of the first year. When the agreed upon time comes to reassess the expenses for the property, a report will be generated showing real expenses and if they show to be more than "base" estimated costs, you, as the tenant, will have to pay the difference.

As an example, if the expenses for the first year are $0.43 psf (per square foot (psf) and the next year it shows to be $0.50 psf, then you would be responsible for $0.07 psf of the expenses.

Full Service Gross Lease

A full service gross lease is at the other end of the spectrum and affords the most protection to you and your practice. All you have to do is pay the rent and all other building operating expenses are paid for by the owner. Because there will be no changes in your rent, you will be able to accurately budget your expenses for the year and know there will be no surprises because you left the heating, ventilating, and air conditioning (HVAC) running day and night for a month. For obvious reasons, most owners don't like these leases because it forces them to absorb the risk of additional costs if something unexpected should occur. Additionally, since you are the one using the electricity and water and gas, it makes an owner uncomfortable that she will be paying for something over which she has no control.

iii. Association Fees

Association fees are exactly the same as CAM fees except they typically exclude property taxes. This is because property taxes are billed directly to the owner of the condo. The first year, the association fees are estimated based on the experience of the management company and the quotes they received from the utility companies. After the first year, the budget is adjusted to reflect the actual costs the building incurred during the year. This adjustment may cause the fees to move up or down depending on the estimated budget's relation to the actual costs.

iv. Warranties

Because I've already talked about this in an early part of this chapter, I'm not going to go over this in detail here. In fact, the main reason I am bringing this topic to light again is because it is such a common question doctors have when they are considering a building. To the point, I can only give you as long and strong a warranty as my contractor gives me. He can only give me as long and strong a warranty as his sub-contractors, the individual trades, give him. Anything else is a risk that you will find most, if not all, developers are not willing to take.

There are ways we have found to "lengthen" the warranty. One of the most effective ways is by waiting until a tenant has occupied a space before dropping the appropriate HVAC unit on the roof. This can be more expensive to the developer because it costs money to bring a crane out and place the units and since HVAC units will have to be in and operating for the common area, the developer would have to pay extra for the crane to come out again. Additionally, the curbs and gutters and landscaping are already installed so you have a great risk of damaging them. Nonetheless, we have done it on several buildings where we expect to have a delay between when the building is completed and when the doctors will occupy their space. This can only be done if you are putting up "package units," all-in-one systems that include the compressor and the fan. A variable air volume (VAV) or other trunk-based system must be installed during the construction of the building.

v. Rent Commencement

Rent commencement refers to the day you start paying rent. If you have already provided your first month's rent, it should be prorated based on the day of the month, with the balance applied to the next month's rent. There are commonly two different ways for rent to begin.

The first way is by having an event trigger the commencement. Opening your practice is the most common event that can trigger rent to start. A close second is when your final inspection has been signed off and you are authorized to occupy your suite. A developer will ask for this type of rent commencement trigger when he is in charge of the tenant improvement construction. Because the developer can only control his contractor but cannot control when you move your furniture in and open for business, he will often insist that the rent commences when he's done with his side of the deal. The city or county inspector signs the permit card, thereby releasing you to start your business. An interesting piece of information to note is that it is very common for the city or county inspector to not allow any non-construction materials, like filing cabinets or desks, on the premises until he has approved the suite and "finaled" the permit card, but that, of course, doesn't include any medical equipment, like chairs or lights, which require direct connection to water, electricity, gas, or compressed air.

The second way is by giving a certain amount of time from some event, namely signing the lease. If a doctor uses his own contractor, I will include in the lease a five-month window for the doctor to design and complete his space. When that five-month window closes the rent begins. I give five months of free rent after the execution of the lease because that is exactly how long it takes me to design and construct a suite if I am running the project and my consultants are designing and constructing the suite. I don't want to be penalized monetarily for the doctor's decision to use his own contractor.

The fact is, I have only known one doctor to complete her space in the allotted five months (and it was really her husband who ran the project). When I interviewed him about the key to his success, he told me it was having the *right team* together. He enthusiastically told me that having a strong designer and well-coordinated contractor was critical to his success and he otherwise would not have been able to finish the project in time. He also pointed out that it required an enormous amount of time on his part.

> I have only known one doctor to complete her space in the allotted five months.

If you are going to use your own team, make sure they have worked together before and have strong experience in medical space construction.

vi. Tenant Improvement Allowance

The tenant improvement allowance is money you receive from the owner to use for designing and building your suite. It will cost more to design and build your suite than the amount the owner gives so you need to plan on paying for the majority of your tenant improvements (TIs) using money from your own sources. The cost to build your suite varies greatly depending on the economy, both local and general, the location, your requirements, and several other factors. It is a waste of your time to ask the owner or broker how much you should expect to pay because what they tell you will be invariably wrong. Doctors always ask and they are always disappointed when it costs more. If you think about whom you are asking you understand why. The broker and developer want you to move into the building, so if they have a range of what they think it might cost, they will tell you the low side so as not to dissuade you.

In actuality, there is absolutely no way for them to know because they don't know what type of finishes you will chose, and they are not contractors who run numbers everyday. Instead of making someone guess what the cost of your tenant improvements will be, focus on moving as quickly as possible to a space plan that works for you and then get a preliminary bid from a couple of contractors you are considering. I will get into that in greater detail later in chapter 4.

Your TI allowance will be based on useable square feet because it deals with your existing area for both the design and the construction. I pay it out as invoiced and use your money first and then my money. Why? Because I know I have my money. In order to make sure your suite will be completed, I will use your money first. Once the amount you are called to put in has been given to me, I know the project will be completed. Often I require the full amount you owe to be given to me, so I can manage it. Why is it important for me to manage it? Because it is my building that gets a lien put on it if you don't pay your contractor and you don't get the proper paperwork returned from your contractor each time you pay him. So we handle all the payments, which generally makes everyone happy. You don't have to deal with another payment every month, and you don't have to ensure all the paperwork is in order. You certainly have enough paperwork and payables to contend with; another one that brings no direct benefit to your company doesn't help. We like handling it because it gives us the ability to protect our property's financial situation. If a contractor puts a lien on our property, not only do you become in default of the lease, but our property also becomes 'unfinanceable'. The situation that arises from property liens is not fun and is worth avoiding. I have never had a problem when I have managed the payments.

> **It is a waste of your time to ask the owner or broker how much you should expect to pay because what they tell you will be invariably wrong.**

Of course, it can make anyone uneasy to hand over thousands of dollars and trust the owner will use it appropriately. This is where good negotiation takes place so you can reach an agreement that makes you feel comfortable with the situation. My advice is this: let the developer handle the payments if he prefers to do it that way, then negotiate a process or procedure that you feel comfortable with.

vii. Construction Management Fees

Construction management fees are becoming more common with developers. It covers the costs of the developer overseeing your project from the design phase through the construction phase. The service will vary greatly, but basically the developer will ensure your architect doesn't design something that is incompatible the existing building, like having a wall end in a window. The construction manager for the owner will also ensure that the contractor doesn't do any damage to the building. The higher-end services will actually run your project for you.

Construction management is of great value, particularly for physicians. This has been repeatedly communicated to me by doctors: the cost of construction management was worth it because of the enormous amount of time and money it saved. Time—because you are not doing something you were not trained to do; money—because you can focus on your practice and seeing patients. The time away from your patients is lost money. There is also time you will lose as your project takes much longer than it would if a professional ran it. You might have guessed: we like to run the projects because we are professionals, and we find that doctors don't like paying rent when they are not operating their business and their rent commencement date has passed. A professional will make sure they are as close to the rent commencement as possible.

THINGS *to* REMEMBER

1. **Don't assume that what a person says or does is the reason they are saying or doing it.**

2. **Don't get distracted by emotions; yours or theirs.**

3. **Positions are what we want. Interests are why we want it.**

4. **The point of understanding the interests of others is not to give them everything they want.**

Chapter Three
FINANCING

Financing is a very personal issue. There are many different scenarios that you will encounter when dealing with financing—whether it be an issue of a partnership, differing financial goals, equity, income, and the number of years that the practice has been running or how long you have been out of med school. All of these play a factor in each situation, but there are fundamentals that are useful for you to understand as you start the process of working out your financing options.

By working through some of the fundamentals now, you will not only save yourself time, but probably some money along the way. Understanding the basics can help you avoid getting started down a false path, which brings me to the first thing I'd like to talk to you about: getting pre-qualified. Often, you'll hear from the finance community that you should get pre-qualified so that you will know how much you can afford and you can negotiate a better bottom line; you can tell the developer or the seller that you can close quickly because you've already been pre-qualified.

The truth of the matter is that pre-qualification is probably more useful for you personally in the sense of being able to make an objective decision. I can tell you, as a developer, there's really little benefit to me whether someone's been pre-qualified. Anyone can get pre-qualified.

From a developer's perspective, any lender (particularly someone you know) will pre-qualify you for some amount. What is of more relevance to a developer is a client who will be able to close quickly, but even your ability to close quickly will only matter to me if I need the money quickly.

The main benefit of getting pre-qualified is to allow yourself an objective, realistic understanding of what you can afford to purchase. This step also allows you to stay fiscally sound as you begin your practice. It will let you know exactly how much down payment you will need. You are going to have another person looking at your life, looking at your financial situation and your financial goals, and telling you, "Look I know that you really want to buy this $2 million space, but you can only afford $1.5 million, so we should either wait until you can afford the $2 million or you should really look somewhere else." I strongly recommend that you listen to this advice. Don't just listen to one person, though. You should listen to several people; we'll get into that in more detail later in this chapter.

> **The main benefit of getting pre-qualified is to allow yourself an objective, realistic understanding of what you can afford to purchase.**

Getting pre-qualified is important, being objective is important. You need to be objective and realistic through this entire process, and financing is certainly one of the areas where you don't want to base your decisions on what you're *hoping will happen*. This is why getting pre-qualified is an important first step.

As a matter of fact, I recommend that you think about getting pre-qualified before looking for a space. That way, you won't be led down the primrose path only to find you can't put a deal together. I've watched several doctors do this and it's unfortunate for them—and it's been unfortunate for me as well. Financial prequalification is important to think about.

What do you need to get pre-qualified? Well, there are a few things that a lender is going to look for:

- Three years of business taxes, if you have an existing practice
- Three years of personal taxes
- A personal financial statement
- Three months of your bank statements

Now, some lenders will ask for additional items and some may not ask for this much. But, if you have these four things in hand, you'll be prepared for what 99 percent of the lenders out there are looking for, so it's a good idea to take the time to get these things together. The records from three years of business taxes are for the businesses that you are in whether it is a corporation or a partnership. Most doctors form partnerships, but whatever the structure of the company you're in, collect the tax records for each of them because at the end of the day the lender wants to see a whole picture of what your life looks like financially.

By looking at this information, lenders can see whether you are a good investment because, from their perspective, that's what they're doing. They're investing money in you based on the statements you make and the financial documents you provide. You want to convince them that you're a low-risk borrower.

They're also going to want to see three years of personal taxes. Now, if you've just come out of med school and you don't really have much to show, that's okay. Show them what you have so they can make a practical assessment of what you can do.

Your personal financial statement is your list of assets and liabilities. There's software for this and there are websites that can help you put together a financial statement, or you can hire someone to help you do it. Often, a bank can walk you through the process. In any case, it is something that you need to do, something all lenders ask for. It really doesn't take that much time. So far then, you have three things you're going to want to look at: three years of business taxes, three years of personal taxes, and your personal financial statements.

Finally, you want to provide three months of bank statements. This provides verification of what you're claiming in your financial statements. If you say that you have $10,000 in liquid assets in a savings account, they want to see that this isn't something that you just went to the local casino and won, but rather that it's something you have had, something reliable. They want to see that you make good financial decisions, and the best way for them to do that is to get a whole picture. Someone who's saving money is often somebody who is more reliable, financially speaking. If you don't show any cash in your accounts and you're running from paycheck to paycheck, that could tell the banks that you might be a risky investment.

During the whole process it's critical that you are honest with the lenders. To get the house you want, you might lie about how much you make or how much your assets are worth, and if the banks don't check that closely you can sometimes get away with it. But, when you're dealing with your business, it's best to look at it clear-eyed and not fool yourself into something that you simply can't afford. There are a lot of people relying on you to be successful. Not just the lender and not just your family, but also the owner of the building who is trusting that you're going to be able to buy the space as you profess, because when you go to escrow, the seller takes the property off the market and can't sell it to somebody else. They'll lose between thirty to sixty days of access to the market for that space because you've committed to buying it and they're trusting that you will, in fact, do that.

Going into escrow is not the time to be figuring out whether you can afford something. That's not fair to the owner. Going into escrow should be a time that you spend looking at the property and deciding if it is what it's been purported to be, if there's anything

> **During the whole process it's critical that you are honest with the lenders.**

wrong with it. You should be very confident that you can put this deal together *before* entering escrow. Likewise with a lease; if you commit your money to a lease, move in, and realize after six months that you can't make it work because you can't make your payments, you're going to be letting a lot of people down. So, it's very important to think all this stuff through. Be honest with yourself about what you're capable of doing.

Additionally, you don't want to commit to leasing the space and start construction, only to find that you don't have enough money to finish the project. At the end of the day it's about doing what you probably already do in your personal life.

Now that you have your three years of business taxes, three years of your personal taxes, your personal financial statements, three months bank statements, in essence you're all dressed up with nowhere to go. How do you find a lender? Probably the best place to start is with the bank that you already use for your daily life. Whether it is a big bank or a small bank, it doesn't matter; the bank you use for personal finances is the one that knows you best. You already have a relationship with them. From a lender's perspective, your loan is an easier "sell" to the people who approve it when you have personal deposits in their bank.

Because of this relationship, the lender is going to be more interested in working with you than someone at a bank that doesn't know you or doesn't have any relationship with you. If you need a loan quickly, using someone with whom you already have a strong relationship is going to be the best way to go. I have heard of lenders funding loans within thirteen days from the time escrow opened. It is unusual, but the point is it was possible because they already had a strong relationship with the client. The client gave the bank a heads-up that they were thinking of going into escrow and so they ordered the appraisal. The bank already had all their financial information and was able to quickly process the loan because of the long-term relationship with the client.

Obviously, in that case, the client didn't need to provide three months of bank statements because the bank was able to just look in the client's file. Things like that can definitely help expedite the process. Going to your personal bank is a wise choice and something that I strongly recommend. If you don't want to spend the time looking at a bunch of banks initially, look to your bank to get pre-qualified. It will give you a good idea of what you're capable of getting from any lender.

If your bank is small, you probably already have a relationship with them. If this is going to be your first practice, the bank will want to establish a long-term relationship with you. Banks make money being a full-service banker, and they will want to have the operating accounts for your business—payroll, business credit cards, an equipment loan, or line of credit for your practice. They want to provide these things because they want to establish a long-term relationship with you and become embedded in your life.

A small bank, typically, can be more creative than a big lender because they're more motivated to keep your business. They understand that they will have a hard time competing with the rates a big lender can offer, so they will go out of their way to be competitive on products and services. It's possible that they can give you a better credit card rate when they couple the equipment loan with your real estate loan. They can work with your line of credit, maybe give you a bigger line of credit than they normally would. The more integrated you are in their services; the better able they are to provide a way of competing with the big banks. The loan officer can say, "Okay, I can't necessarily give you the best rate that you could find on the loan for this real estate. But, I can give you a very low interest rate on your credit card, I can give you a better-than-the-competition rate on your equipment loan, and I can give you a bigger line of credit than another bank would be able to. Perhaps we can throw in payroll processing for free for several months, or we can give you some type of strong services on your operating accounts."

This is definitely something to consider when you are dealing with a small bank. And, much like anything in life, per the Western philosophy, we often think of the bottom line and we lose focus on the whole picture. One of the great benefits of working with Asian countries, particularly the Chinese, is that they teach you that there's a bigger picture to be aware of. When you're in negotiations, when you're looking at making a decision as to which bank to use for your loan, it's important to focus on more than the interest rate or the monthly payment. Of course, that's important; at the end of the day you're going to have to make the payments and they need to be affordable. But, if you've been honest and forthright with the bank about what you can afford, you'll find that there's really going to be some give in that end number.

When you find the project you're most interested in, you'll find out what the "common area and maintenance fees" and the monthly utilities will cost. Using these numbers, you can develop a better understanding of your overall costs. The bank will point out these details and tell you what the typical industry standard is and what to expect. A broker is an even better source of information for those particular items, which you can plug into your cash flow analysis; however, the banks will have a good idea of what those costs are because they're putting deals together all the time. Their numbers won't be too far off. I do think that a broker is a better source, or, if you have a particular building that you're looking at, talk directly with the developer. The owner is the best source for knowing how much it costs to operate in his building—you can often request a budget showing actual operating costs. This will give you a good idea of what you'll have to pay on a month-to-month basis.

Even if you don't use all the full-service offerings of a small bank, you'll find that it will be more creative than a large bank; the market will generally force them to do this. But large or small, any lender will want to see a 1.25 debt service. In other words, they'll want to see that you're bringing in 25 percent more than what you're going to owe each month on the loan and that you're not asking for more than 80 percent of the value of whatever you're trying to buy, otherwise known as the loan-to-value or LTV.

That's the way a typical conventional loan is set up. You will find, however, that a smaller bank can make more creative loans. There will be times when you find what's called a 90 percent conventional. A 90 percent conventional refers to a 90 percent loan-to-value. So, if the building or property you're looking at is worth $1 million, they will be able to give you a loan up to $900,000 and you would have to come up with $100,000. Because there's a higher loan to value and the bank is more at risk if you default, they will typically want to see a 1.5 debt service. In other words, they will want to see that your revenue shows 50 percent of what you would have to pay on the loan.

> ◆
>
> **You will find, however, that a smaller bank can make more creative loans.**
>
> ◆

If your company is very strong, has a lot of cash flow, and your practice is successful, this might be a way of acquiring a loan without having to use the Small Business Administration (SBA). And there are times when you won't meet the qualifications of the SBA. While there are many determinations that factor into whether your company is considered a small business by the government, one item is your gross annual revenue. If your company is receiving revenue of more than $6.5 million a year, it is not considered a small business. In that case, a 90 percent conventional loan would still give you the same financing structure, but would not provide you the benefits of a SBA loan.

One of the downfalls of a small bank is that they will not have as competitive interest rates. Their rates will generally be higher. The other downfall is the available capital. They will have certain limitations on how much capital they can put out, and your loan may exceed the amount they can put forth. In that case you would have to find a lender that has more available capital, most likely a bigger lender. Banks such as Bank of America have a medical department that specializes in loans to doctors. They also have more competitive rates because they're competing not only with the big lenders, but they're competing with all the small lenders as well, so their competition base is larger. Additionally, they are able to be more competitive because they have more available capital.

Big lenders will be able to give you more money because they have more capital to draw from. Another benefit of a big lender is that they will often have a medical division that focuses solely on loans to doctors for their practices. Because of this, it is possible to get small bank service from a large bank. In essence, it is a financing company inside of a financing company.

What is the best plan of attack when you're going out to find a bank? My recommendation is to initially go to five banks. The first bank should be your personal bank (we've discussed all the benefits of this). The second place I recommend is the large banks you've had initial conversations with. You should feel comfortable with their view of your practice, the possibilities of what you're trying to do, whether it is something within their scope of financing and something they can support. If you have to explain all the intricate details because they don't understand what you're talking about, you should look for a different large bank.

> My recommendation is to initially go to five banks.

Finally, I recommend going to a few mid-sized community banks in your area. Interview them, talk to the person you'd be interacting with, and make sure you feel comfortable with their level of expertise. Don't be shy in asking how long they've been doing loans, how long they've been working at the bank, and what their experience level is. Feel free to ask them any detailed questions about SBA loans, how many SBA loans they've done that year, etc. Really query them until you feel comfortable with them. If you find that their answers aren't adequate, I strongly recommend that you move on. Even if you feel that you've exhausted all your possibilities, I still recommend that you work only with a bank with whom you feel comfortable.

The five banks will provide you with the broadest scope of the financial market available to you without getting overly complicated. If you go to more than five banks, it becomes very difficult to track, and it's time consuming. Generally, I've found that querying five banks allows you to get a good idea of what's available in the market. You can compare their answers and determine which lender you feel the most comfortable with. The important part in determining the lender is not just the rates that you get from them. Generally, the questions they get are: what is the rate, and how much can you lend me? While these are important, there are other important considerations. For instance, if the lender can't fund the loan when the time comes to close escrow, the interest rate or loan amount is not going to matter much.

It's critical that you get a clear picture of how well a bank performs. An excellent way of doing this is to ask to speak with clients that have been with them for a long time or that have recently done deals with them within the last month, specifically with the person you're working with as well as the underwriter that your loan officer will be working with. If you find that they take longer than they promise, you may go down a path that will ultimately lead to the demise of the deal. Keep this in mind when you're judging the lender. Referrals are probably the best way to avoid a bad lender.

How much time should you plan on taking to get all this work done? I recommend that you plan for the following:

One month to put together the financial statements, gathering your tax returns, all the things that we've discussed and getting your pre-qualifications.

During this month you will also spend time finding a lender. It shouldn't take more than a week to gather your financial statements, your tax returns, your financial statements, three months of bank statements, and your business and personal taxes for the past three years.

After that, take a week to contact the banks and start interviews, talking to the different lenders that might be helpful to you.

At the end of that week, submit your financials to each of them and ask for a commitment letter within two weeks. They should be able to underwrite at least on your personal side, and be able to say that they can put a loan together for you within two weeks, particularly if you give them all the financial information listed here.

This will allow you to be pre-qualified so that you'll know exactly what you *can* do and what you *can't* do. At the end of that month, you should plan for a one to two month escrow. It's during the escrow that there are several occasions when you can get delayed. There are things that will need to be done during the escrow in order for the loan to close:

An environmental report will have to be generated.

The underwriting will have to be completed. There will have to be an appraisal done for the property and/or loan.

This all takes time, with the appraisal generally taking the longest period of time, usually three to four weeks. The environmental report will generally take one to two weeks, and the underwriting can be accomplished in that same period of time—one to two weeks.

It's important to get the appraisal ordered immediately once you enter escrow because it will take longer than everything else that needs to be done in order to fund your loan. If you do, and everything is in order, it's very possible for you to do a 30-day escrow. Generally you'll want to ask for a 45- to 60-day escrow, but if the owner is demanding a 30-day escrow or you need a 30-day escrow for special reasons, it is definitely possible, if you have everything in order.

Delays in Escrow

Where can you be delayed along the way in escrow? The most common way is by not providing all the information the lender needs. Sometimes, that won't be your fault—it could be that the lender didn't ask all the questions, or provide all the information needed along the way. At the end of the process when it becomes an emergency, the lender may realize he doesn't have a piece of information he needs. You'll find that you can avoid these types of lenders by asking for references, speaking to their clients, and asking their clients how that process went. For instance, ask, "Was the lender thorough in the questions that he asked and the information that he requested? Or, did he force you to jump through several hoops at the end of the process and run a bunch of fire drills to get the deal done?"

Another common cause of delay during the process of escrow is the appraisal. If you include your tenant improvements costs as part of the loan process, those costs will have to be factored in by the appraiser when he is looking at the value of the property. He will typically require that you provide plans and specifications for what you intend to build. If you haven't completed these plans, you will significantly delay the process. If you intend on including your tenant improvements in the loan, you should expect to have those reviewed by the appraiser; you'll have to submit them before the loan is closed. This is commonly not understood and is frequently a source of delay as escrow comes to a close.

By the plans and specifications I mean: what you intend to build and what types of finishes you will use. A preliminary pricing plan should be sufficient in accomplishing this task. You'll submit the preliminary pricing plan to the appraiser as well as the bid, which the preliminary pricing plan was based on. You should also give the appraiser your contractor's bid because the bid shows the value of your tenant improvements and should persuade the appraiser to give you full credit for the cost of the tenant improvements.

For instance, if the contractor's bid comes in at $300,000 and the appraiser wants to show that your tenant improvements are valued at $200,000, the contractor's bid will give you a strong argument that $300,000 is the current market for the tenant improvements that you intend on building. Quite frequently, the lender will ask to see the plans and specifications so you should be prepared to provide both documents to the lender during the process of the loan.

The environmental report is an additional document that looks at the environmental history of the property. You will need to provide an updated environmental report. Generally, this is provided by the owner of the property. He will give you an updated report that shows the use on the site, any environmental findings on the site and 99 percent of the time you'll find that it is clear and contains no issues. But, this is required by all SBA lenders, and most conventional lenders as well. It will take one to two weeks to provide, so order it right away. If the lender waits to order this, it can delay closing escrow. They won't be able to close the loan without it.

Finally, underwriting can be a source of delay. Here is something very important for you to ask when you're talking to different lenders. There are three different types of lenders that work with the SBA. There's a preferred lending program (PLP), a certified lending program (CPL), and a general program (GP). These are part of different programs that function under the SBA loan program. You want to work with a preferred lender who's operating under the preferred lending program. These lenders have processed *many* loans through the SBA; they've gone beyond being certified and are fully trusted by the SBA to underwrite the loan. They do not have to look to the SBA to underwrite the loan or review any of the underwriting, and can, therefore, process the loan much more quickly. Using a preferred lender will generally save you two weeks. There really isn't much of a benefit to using a certified lender, except that you might get a better rate; they realize they won't be able to be as performance oriented as a preferred lender. But in the end you could very well pay for it in the delays it will cause. My recommendation is to use a preferred lender.

> ◆
> **You want to work with a preferred lender who's operating under the preferred lending program.**
> ◆

A certified lender has to submit their underwriting to the SBA, which will then confirm the underwriting, perform any other necessary reviews, ask any other follow up questions to the lender, and ultimately will either approve or disapprove the underwriting. The certified lender will not be able to fund the loan until they've received that approval from the SBA, which can take up to two weeks.

A general lender who functions under the general lending program does not do any of the underwriting. They rely solely upon the SBA to do all the underwriting and, therefore, the delay can be even greater. Unless there is an overwhelming reason to use a certified lender or a general lender, the preferred lender is certainly the most professional, the most experienced, and should be the best performer—all compelling reasons to choose one.

SBA

An SBA loan is the most common way a small business finances a project, whether it be for lease or equipment acquisition or property acquisition. While the most common interactions are in loans, the SBA actually provides many services, including disaster assistance, online training, counseling, and various contract opportunities. They also can help you understand laws and regulations. They are a government agency, and are backed and funded by the government.

A little about the SBA; it was created in 1953. Its goal is to look out for the interest of small businesses, recognizing that small business is a critical element in the U.S. economy. It was established to ensure that small businesses have opportunities to grow and become more successful. It is through small businesses that the United States is able to compete on a global level. By ensuring that small businesses succeed we can enjoy stability in our economy.

The way that you'll most often interact with the SBA is through your lender. Lenders have a partnership with the SBA that gives them opportunities to provide services to you they wouldn't otherwise be able to provide. There are two types of loans that you'll typically consider when you are looking at an SBA loan. There's a 7A and there's a 504.

The 7A is a government secured loan; they don't actually provide any capital, but rather guarantee up to 75 percent of the loan. From the perspective of the lender, this is considered a secured loan because the government is backing it. If the government didn't agree to back it, the lender may not be willing to absorb all the risk.

So, a government-backed loan reduces significant portions of risk to the lender because they know, at a minimum, 75 percent of the loan that they've issued you can be recovered from the government should you default.

Most often the 7A loans are used for working capital. While working capital is technically defined as your current assets minus your current liabilities, from a real-world perspective working capital is your ability to cover your debts. That can also include any assets that you have as inventory, but you'll most often find it in your accounts receivables and the cash that you have. What this means is you'll be able to take a loan that will allow you to operate your business.

Another reason to use a 7A program from the SBA is for your tenant improvements. This would be if you were leasing a space rather than buying. Because your tenant improvements don't improve your space, but instead improve value to the landlord, you typically would use a 7A loan to improve that space. Obviously, you need to improve the space in order to operate your business, but the real value is added to the building itself and not your practice. Those tenant improvements become part of the building and you do not own them. You're simply agreeing to use them while you are occupying the space. Once you leave the space, those improvements will remain and be considered part of the building; you will not be able to take them. Because of the tenant improvement's temporary nature a 7A loan would be applicable to this type of situation.

You can also use a 7A loan to buy land or buildings. Your financial situation will determine whether a 7A loan would make sense to buy real estate because this is not a typical loan for land or building acquisitions. It is far more useful for leases when you need money to do your tenant improvements, to start operating your business, or for operational costs. The only reason you might want to use a 7A loan for land or building acquisition is if you plan on selling it shortly after you have purchased it.

A 7A loan is structured as a variable rate linked to the prime rate. It generally matures or is due at the end of ten years. Often, it can be amortized based on a ten-year term, as opposed to a 504 loan that uses a fixed rate, is tied to the T-Bill, and is a fully amortized twenty-five-year loan. The reason you'd want to use a 504 loan to buy land or to buy equipment is because the equipment and the land will be utilized for long periods of time. Typically, the equipment won't last as long as the land or building. But the generally accepted industry way of viewing the acquisition of land or building is as a long-term hold. Land or building acquisition is where a 504 loan is strongly recommended.

The 504 loan is a property-secured loan as opposed to a government-secured loan, like the 7A. If you should default on a 504 loan, the lender will have the right to take the property back. Because this is typically used for land or a building and one of the conditions to a 504 loan is that it must be "owner occupied." This means you must occupy 51 percent of the building you are using the 504 loan to acquire. So, in the situation where you are not going to be occupying 51 percent, a 7A loan would be more useful and may be the only way you could acquire the building under the SBA loan program.

While both loans are useful for different scenarios, you typically want to use a 7A loan for short-term or transient acquisitions, such as things that don't bring value to your property but bring value to something else, such as your profitability or productivity. The tenant improvements would be a transient acquisition that you ultimately do not benefit from and would not be able to take with you.

In the 504 case, for an equipment acquisition you would be able to take the equipment with you after you vacate the premises should you be leasing, so even if you do lease you could use a 504 to purchase the equipment. In the case where you were moving into a suite that already had tenant improvements built out, you could use a 504 loan to acquire your necessary equipment because you would be able to take it with you. Additionally, with the 504, the main focuses will be on the property because it will be secured. Additionally, if you use it for an equipment acquisition the lender will secure the loan through the equipment. If you default, the equipment will become the property of the lender.

The final question you should ask yourself when considering your financing is, ultimately, what type of property you want and whether you want to lease or buy. The market-specific demands will determine the answer to that question. In most cases, in thriving areas with lots of available patients, you will find that, in the end, you'll spend less to buy the space than you would to lease the space. Many doctors have found this to be true and have looked to either purchase their own building or to purchase a condo within a building. As condominiums become more available, and become a product more widely accepted by the medical and dental community, they will allow a small business owner to be able to own their own space in an area or situation where they otherwise wouldn't be able.

It is my strong recommendation that you thoroughly look at the possibility of owning a property as opposed to leasing. I consider leasing to be secondary in value to purchasing and I'm sure you'd agree, which is why most of America values owning a home as opposed to leasing a residence. As much as condos have enabled many people to be owners in real estate on the residential side, so I believe as time goes on condos will enable doctors and business people to own the space they occupy, and reap the financial and community-driven benefits.

> **It is my strong recommendation that you thoroughly look at the possibility of owning a property as opposed to leasing.**

THINGS *to* REMEMBER

1 **Get Pre-Qualified**

2 **Be honest with the lenders *and* yourself**

3 **Use a *preferred* SBA *lender***

Chapter Four

SPACE PLANNING AND CONSTRUCTION DRAWINGS IN THREE MONTHS OR LESS

Space planning is the easiest way to lose money. I have watched doctors spend several months space planning a suite, not realizing they are losing thousands of dollars because they are "off schedule," which means that rent will commence prior to the practice operating.

They are also losing money because every day a practice doesn't operate, the money it could have made is lost forever; you can't get back patient visits. And you can't market your space because you really don't know when it will open. If you have marketed your practice but miss the "opening" date, you are actually worse off than if you had not marketed it at all. All the momentum disappears and worse yet, your "news" is no longer new and exciting.

If you are forced to re-market your practice because of missing your planned opening date, the original people you targeted with your marketing may no longer care, or, worse yet, the desire you created by telling them about your service prompted them to find another doctor when calls to your practice yielded no response. Bottom line, you lose.

Don't squander the precious time you have to design and build your suite! Five months will disappear in an instant, and three of those months will be spent designing and permitting your space. Get your team together and get to work. Establish a schedule with the architect and contractor. If you don't have a schedule, you will not be successful in opening your practice at the five-month mark, which is the amount of time planning and building your suite should not exceed. "What if I have seven months before my rent starts?" you might ask. My answer is, "Then get two months of free rent *while* you are operating." I understand that space planning will pull you away from your love of taking care of your patients. It is difficult justifying spending your time on something that doesn't generate any money. But this is more about not *losing* money, and you need to keep that in mind throughout the hours of tedious work that go into looking at plans and coordinating with architects and the city and your contractor. The good news is that once you finalize the space plan you'll be able to rest a bit as the engineers and architect completes the working drawings, which will be submitted to the city or county for plan check and permits. Of course, you will have to continually follow up to ensure they are staying on schedule.

Many doctors have expressed confusion about the difference between the space plan and working drawings. Space plans show how your suite will be laid out in the space allocated to you. It shows where each room will be located and becomes the foundation for all the other thirty sheets of paper, which will comprise your working drawings. It is easy to change the space plan when there are no working drawings. Once you have working drawings, it becomes far more difficult to make modifications to the plans. You might have had experience with this when remodeling or building your house. This is the same. You cannot build the suite with the space

> **Every day a practice doesn't operate, the money it could have made is lost forever; you can't get back patient visits.**

plan without a great deal of interpretation on your contractor's part, something you should avoid like the plague.

The working drawings include what are called "details," and they are exactly that—very detailed drawings of how to construct the walls, how the walls connect to the floor, how the ceiling connects to the building, and so on. They will also include the line drawings for both the plumbing and electrical and show precisely their coordination with the building system, the amps each will carry, transformers in the line, etc. There are rural areas that will let you submit space plans with written details and they will approve them. Even in these rare cases, though, I would recommend against it. A full set of working drawings will ensure everything is built according to industry standards and government code. You will avoid many arguments with your contractor and, with a good set of drawings and a clear line of communication, there will be no room for interpretation—the contractor can't give you a "change order" while under construction. (In the construction chapter I discuss how to pick a contractor and what to watch out for.)

> **Don't squander the precious time you have to design and build your suite!**

There is an important point I should make here. You need to stop and consider how you plan on handling the construction bidding process. If you are going to use one contractor and accept whatever bid he gives you, you can save money and do a design-build style mechanical, engineering, and plumbing (MEP) drawing. This style of design is called design-build because the person who designs it will also be the person who builds it. That can be very good from a responsibility perspective. If the same person who designs it also builds it, you only have to talk to one person. On the other hand, when one person designs it and another person builds it, you have to play judge and jury.

When you play judge and jury between two or more parties, there is only one way to do it: bring all the appropriate parties together in one room or in a phone conference. It might take you a day or two to figure out exactly who is appropriate because people are going to be pointing fingers.

You will waste considerable time if you talk to each person individually. And it is still very possible you will never come to a solution. I strongly recommend that you have this meeting in person. There is a powerful psychological phenomenon that occurs when people are facing each other. There is significantly less posturing and more interest in coming to an agreeable solution for all parties.

Now that I've convinced you to use a design-build method, I should tell you that what you gain in focused responsibility you will lose in bidding accountability. When you award someone a design-build contract all competition gets thrown out the window. They no longer have to beat anyone else's prices so they'll often give you a price that they know won't set off alarms, but it will not be the best price. If you want their best price, you are going to have to bid the project to several subcontractors in that trade. The only practical and professional way to do this is to hire an engineer to design the system, such as plumbing, for example. Once those have been finalized and verified in coordination with the architect, they should be given to the contractor who will send it out to three subcontractors. It should only take a week for the sub-contractors to return a hard bid to the general contractor.

> A full set of working drawings will ensure everything is built according to industry standards and government code.

In order to stay on schedule to finish your suite within five months you must closely monitor the time you spend in the space planning phase. Make a commitment to yourself that you will answer any questions from your architect the same day. That includes questions you receive at night. If you are capable of making a decision at that time, then get the answer back to the architect immediately. Focus begets focus. If your consultants see that you are responding immediately to their questions, you will be letting them know that what they are doing is a priority to you. This helps ensure a focused team that will complete the project quickly.

To stay on schedule, you will need to complete your space plan within one month. If you go over a month, everything will be pushed back. Put a schedule in your contract with your architect. Have an agreed upon timeline, spelling out exactly how quickly you expect her to respond to your changes and, after she submits the working drawings, the changes requested by the city. Give her financial incentives to meet those deadlines, and financially penalize her if she gets behind schedule. It will take discernment and you will have to be graceful, but having this schedule in place will keep everyone focused on the goal without you having to call every hour to check up on them.

When you finalize the space plan, it will be sent to the engineers who will design their systems based on the shell building drawings and the space plan. In addition to the working drawings, the electrical engineer will propose light fixtures and provide "cut sheets" or specification sheets that also typically have pictures of the fixture if the architect hasn't proposed one in the space plan specifications. I will frequently get suggestions from my engineer on other light fixtures that look similar to the architect's proposed fixture but costs considerably less. Commit to deciding on these specifications quickly, within a day.

> There is a powerful psychological phenomenon that occurs when people are facing each other.

– How the Space Plan and Working Drawing Process Should Go –

Space Plan
Preliminary Pricing Plan
Working Drawings

Space Plan

As I mentioned, the point of the space plan is to organize your space so that it is functional for your practice. A good space planner will have already done hundreds of these projects in the past and will understand what you need, probably as soon as you tell them your specialty. The dirty little secret in space planning is this: while most doctors spend weeks laying out their space and making sure the adjacencies are correct, they usually end up organizing their space almost exactly how the space planner would have designed it without any input. Everyone, including me, likes to think they have unique needs, that their needs are atypical, that their needs demand special consideration and attention. The truth is most offices for a particular specialty are designed very similarly because there are only so many ways to design a space. The size of the suite does not change the truth of what I just said; it just demands more replication of the same kind of room, or a larger version of the room. More examination rooms, a larger nurses station, an insurance consultant, all these can be added or subtracted to adjust to the size of the suite. My recommendation is to first find a good space planner that has many years of dental or medical space planning experience, and then tell him or her what you need.

Normally, you supply this information at what is called a "programming meeting." At this meeting, you will tell the space planner how many people will be working in your office, what their roles are, how many exam rooms or how many chairs you'll need, and any special equipment you will include in your suite. Because you are successful and driven, you will have to fight your tendency to tell the space planner how to lay out the suite. Don't do it! Instead, let the space planner take the above information, as well as anything else he deems important, and come back to you with a space plan.

The very good space planners will draw something for you at the programming meeting, something you can take home and mull

> ♦
> **If you want their best price, you are going to have to bid the project to several subcontractors in that trade.**
> ♦

> ♦
> **If you go over a month, everything will be pushed back.**
> ♦

over. But don't expect this to be the case. Often they will end the meeting having solely gathered information and given you a commitment to return a space plan to you within a few days. But keep in mind that the ability to design a suite on the spot is not the only way to judge whether a designer is good or not. I have met several excellent designers who, because of their personalities and desire to be thorough, prefer to not draw at the meeting but rather go back to their office and take some time to determine the best way of laying out your suite.

> ◆
>
> **Make a commitment to yourself that you will answer any questions from your architect the same day.**
>
> ◆

When you do get the first space plan, consider why he placed certain rooms next to each other. Even if you have run a successful practice before and you know what works for you, is it possible he might have come up with a better idea? If you have taken your time and chosen wisely, you will have picked a space planner who has designed many suites for the same specialty as yours. Be open minded to the ideas he presents. He has most likely found, after many years of designing specialty medical offices and getting feedback from the doctors who used them, that there are better ways to lay out a space. Therefore, it's worth your time to consider the space plan you receive even if it isn't exactly what you envisioned or how your current practice functions.

> ◆
>
> **Because you are successful and driven, you will have to fight your tendency to tell the space planner how to lay out the suite. Don't do it!**
>
> ◆

When I was studying jazz composition many years ago, my teacher told me, "People know what they like. But more importantly, they like what they know." Keep this in mind as you react to the drawings.

This part of the space planning process should take you no more than two weeks to finish. Committing the time now will ensure that you can complete the project quickly. As I mentioned before, make sure you respond on the *same day* to any drawings, comments or questions you receive, and make sure that the people who will be reviewing it make that same commitment to you as well. It may be that you need a couple of days to think about the drawings. That is fine if you are handed the drawings on Friday. You can then take the weekend to review them. If the nurses or hygienists need to give you input, schedule a meeting and sit down with them.

> ◆ **Be open minded to the ideas he presents.** ◆

My recommendation is give yourself no more than fifteen minutes to meet with them and go over the plans. First, the short time frame will force everyone to concentrate on plans and not begin talking about other things that are on their minds. Second, if it takes longer than that to look at the drawings and decide whether it works or not, you have done one of three things:

1. Not picked the right space planner
2. Are not keeping an open mind
3. Have tried to pack too much into your space

Number three usually happens when you can't afford the space you really want. So you get a smaller space and try to jam more than will fit into it.

Every office is going to have essential elements. While a game room is not an essential element to a successful practice, a compressor is critical for a dentist, and everyone needs a waiting room sized relative to the overall size of your suite. If the owner is willing, and the building can accommodate it, place your compressor in a different location of the building. I often see it placed on the roof on an isolation pad. This can allow you to gain some space.

> ◆ **Before you commit to a building, and the people who own it, make sure you can fit in it.** ◆

Before you commit to a building, and the people who own it, make sure you can fit in it. This is where our previous discussion on financing can play a role. It may be that you can't afford the building and would be better off finding a space that doesn't hinder your practice or its eventual need to grow.

Preliminary Pricing Plan

At the end of two weeks, you should have a space plan that is ninty-five percent finished. The remaining five percent will be decided when you move through the working drawings. This is the point where it might be wise to generate a preliminary pricing plan. A preliminary pricing plan is a space plan with additional information that a contractor can use to give a fairly accurate estimate of how much it will cost to build your suite. It should not take more than one week for your space planner to generate a preliminary pricing plan and it should not take more than one week for your contractor to give you an estimate that is based on this plan. When I handle the tenant improvements for the doctor, I guarantee that the final bid will be within ten percent of the preliminary pricing estimate, if no changes are made to the plans, and that is a reasonable expectation for you to have of your contractor's final numbers.

> You should expect your architect and engineers to take no more than one week to make the city required adjustments to the plans and resubmit them for their second plan check.

Working Drawings

Once the space plan is completed and approved, the architect will begin working drawings. Working drawings should be completed within four weeks, including the engineering drawings. At this point your architect will submit your drawings to the city and begin the plan check process. You should expect the city to take roughly two weeks to return their initial plan check comments to the architect. You should expect your architect and engineers to take no more than one week to make the city required adjustments to the plans and resubmit them for their second plan check. In the worst case scenario, it should not take more than three plan checks for the city to approve the plans. If it takes more than rounds of corrections, you are experiencing a breakdown in communication.

When I have seen this take place it has usually been because the city continues to require changes that it could have required during the first plan check. It is imperative that you insert yourself into the process, go down to the city and meet with plan checker. As I have mentioned before, it is very important that you hear both sides of any story you are trying to judge. Just because the architect is telling you that it is the city's fault for why he has had to resubmit plans 4 times does not mean that is true, and the only way to figure out the truth is to sit everyone down, the architect and engineers and plan checker, and talk about where the failure in communication is occurring.

> **If you don't have time to interview the space planner's references, I would insist that the principal (and only the principal) work on your project.**

Finding an Architect

Because the architect will be your point person throughout the entire project, and because you will rely upon him more than any other person, it is critically important you connect with the right architect. Keep in mind that the right architect for you will not necessarily be the right architect for your colleague, so take your time and be diligent about finding the right one.

There are three ways you can find an architect:

1. Internet
2. Contractor
3. Peers

The Internet

The Internet is a powerful way to find an architect, but you won't have much luck if you actually use the word "architect" while searching. "Space planner" is the keyword you want to use when doing your search. My recommendation would be to use a local city as an additional qualifier. You will need to meet with your planner several times over the course of the first month and frequently thereafter. Additionally you will want your planner to visit the construction site and review the progress of work. Using a search phrase like "Phoenix medical space planner," will be your best chance at finding the appropriate expert who is nearby. Then ask the same common-sense questions you would ask anyone else:

> ◆ The most ideal situation is that the architect and the contractor have worked together. ◆

- How many years have you been designing medical office space?
- How many offices do you design a year?
- Will you personally be working on my project, or will your employees be doing the bulk of the work?
- Who will attend the design meetings?
- Will you work with the engineers to coordinate their drawings and ensure they match your drawings?
- Will you submit both the engineer plans and your plans to the city?
- Will you be the sole point person on the project, such that all communication, all meeting scheduling, all deadline enforcement, all plan submission happens through you?

I have used some amazing space planners before and then fired them in the middle of a project. I have also never used seasoned space planners again after finishing a project. In both situations it was because once I got past the space planner and had to deal with his staff, the quality and timeliness of service went downhill dramatically. If you don't have time to interview the space planner's references, I would insist that the principal (and only the principal) work on your project. He can rely on whomever he wants to help him but you will only talk to him and when you call him only he will call you back. If he doesn't like this proposal, be glad you found out and move on to the next space planner. It isn't worth the gamble.

Contractor

Several doctors have reported success using their contractor as a source for finding an architect. Since the contractor and the architect work in concert through the project, it is critical they work well together. The contractor is the one who must build what the architect communicates through his working drawings.

This, of course, is only useful if you already have a contractor. I have known many doctors who have already had experience with a contractor at a previous location or have found one through the suggestion of a broker, developer, or a friend. If you don't have a contractor, you'll find tips on how to choose one, and the important questions to ask, in the next chapter.

Regardless of how you got to this trustworthy contractor, the most ideal situation is that the architect and the contractor have worked together. This will ensure that the architect and the contractor will have accurate expectations of each other. The architect will have received on-site feedback from the contractor on his proposed details, and the contractor will have already received responses to his requests for clarifications (RFCs). These clarifications will often come in the form of a bulletin or single sheet of paper that has a clarifying or alternative detail for the contractor to use. While the architect always strives for accuracy and cohesion in his drawings, at times it will be necessary to redesign a detail because something out in the field has caused

─────── ◆ ───────

Don't try to make the space planner become something she isn't.

─────── ◆ ───────

the original detail to not work. This is very common and is to be expected on every project.

Plans vary greatly in their attention to detail, and a good contractor will be able to look at a set of drawings and tell you their thoroughness. Keep in mind: some unethical contractors will look for vague elements in a set of plans and bid low for the project, knowing this provides opportunities to upcharge the client during the construction phase. So this method is only useful if you know you have a contractor you can trust. Caveat emptor.

Peers

Peers can be a valid source of finding a space planner so long as you handle it similarly to how you would handle finding a space planner through the Internet. Simply because someone found a space planner to be adequate or even the "best space planner" should not dissuade you from thoroughly questioning the space planner to ensure you are getting one that fits the way you like to do things. The credibility of your peer should never trump your intuition and judgment.

What makes for a good architect or space planner?

First of all, they need to be good listeners. If you have to keep explaining to the space planner that you want three exam rooms and she keeps putting in five, you know you have a problem. My recommendation is this: give them two chances. If they don't get it clearly the second time, then it's clear you two are incompatible when it comes to communication. Don't try to make the space planner become something she isn't. If she doesn't understand what you are looking for, move on, and quickly; you don't have much time. I, too, have been in a situation where I really wanted to make it work with a consultant and it was difficult to recognize and admit that we didn't work well together. It is human nature to want to give someone the benefit of the doubt, but I can tell you that, in the end, I have been right more times than wrong about firing someone. It is simply something that needs to be done when the relationship is not working.

THINGS *to* REMEMBER

1. **Answer questions from your architect the same day.**

2. **Fight your desires to tell your architect how to design your suites.**

3. **The ideal situation is for the architect and the contractor to have worked together before.**

Chapter Five

CONSTRUCTION

Finding the Right Contractor

There are many qualities that define a good contractor. One of the key elements is someone who asks a lot of questions about the drawings. No matter how good an architect is, the communication that occurs through a line drawing is, generally, never complete. While the architect may draw something that is thorough and detailed, it will still rely on the interpretation of the contractor to correctly apply it.

Ideally, you're going to have a contractor who will, in writing, be asking several questions of the architect regarding the plans: looking at the plumbing, the mechanical, the electrical, details of the walls, and even the locations of outlets or if a wall "dies" into a window mullion. If you have a contractor who's looking that thoroughly, and asking questions, you know that you've got a knowledgeable, honest contractor—and one who's not going to come back to you for unwarranted change orders down the road.

Change orders are probably the easiest way contractors make their money. They'll low bid, get the job, and come back and upcharge you as they go, claiming that the plans weren't very clear. They will say also that they assumed you wanted the "cheaper" way, and coming back to you saying, "Now I realize you want it this way, which is far more expensive."

You want all of these considerations to happen during the bidding process. That's when you're going to be able to judge the different contractors you're considering. We're going to get into the bidding process itself in a later section, but the communications between the contractor and the architect will be the most important communication factor for you during this process. It can make the process go very smoothly, or it can make the process extremely challenging, time consuming and something that you'll look back upon hoping to never repeat. This is what we want to avoid.

> **Change orders are probably the easiest way contractors make their money.**

One of the first keys is to have the contractor asking a *lot* of questions about the drawings and thoroughly analyzing them in a way that makes you feel comfortable that he understands the plans. If a contractor is not asking questions, they're probably not looking at the plans closely enough to be able to give you an accurate assessment of them. The contractor, as we've discussed, is the one whose feet are on the ground, hands are on the tools, putting together what the architect is, at times, "guessing" will work. The architect, through experience, has come to understand that the details he uses work better than others and/or that the cities typically like to see these types of details. That's all fine and dandy, but just like any academic exercise, it's the guys out in the field implementing the theories that put them to the true test.

If a contractor looks at something and says, "That's just not going to work," or "Did you go out on site and look at the situation? If you had, you would have noticed that you clearly can't do this because there's a building stairwell in the middle of your hallway. You may want to rethink this," be grateful. Those types of conversations are very important.

The Payment Process

Another element that is important for contractors to understand is the payment process you've decided upon. You need to disclose this up front as you interview the contractors you're considering. Let them know how you will pay them.

First of all, talk about the way the payments will be issued. You want to pay them based their progress. If they've done 10 percent of the work, then you'll be paying them 10 percent of the total contract. Depending on how you have your payments structured, you can either pay them weekly or every couple of weeks or monthly. As a development company (because of all the payments we have to deal with, and the necessary coordinating with the lender), we pay the contractors every thirty days. We have agreements that contractors must have progress invoices submitted at a certain time of the month. If they submit the invoices by the monthly deadline, we pay them within ten days of the deadline.

You do not want to pay contractors up front. Sometimes, they'll insist on getting payment for materials in advance. Generally, we do *not* pay for any materials or any work up front. We expect the contractor to cover that. We will pay them after the first progress invoice has been submitted. If they're asking for payments up front, that tells you that they're a very small operation and/or that they haven't been around for very long, or that they don't know how to manage their money, or that something "negative" has happened in their business recently. You have to consider whether that's someone you'd want to have on your project, and whether he will be around after he has completed the project.

> **We do *not* pay for any materials or any work up front.**

You are going to have issues that come up after the project is completed—a leaky faucet, non-functioning electrical outlet, a door that needs to be adjusted. It's critical that your contractor be able to come back in three, four, five months, or whenever the inevitable problems surface as you start operating your practice. There are always little things that need tweaking. This is why you want a reputable contractor. You don't want a contractor that you're not going to be able to find once the job is done because they don't manage their money well.

Keep that in mind. If a contractor is looking for something up front, move on and interview the next one. The architect should be able to recommend someone. Using your architect to help you filter the pool of contractors can be helpful. If you rely on a peer's suggestion, or information you find online, you'll want to talk about these issues as you're initially querying them.

My recommendation for finding a good contractor is to use the contractor to find the architect or the architect to find the contractor. If you have a good architect that you feel very comfortable with, talk to that architect about what contractors she suggests and has experience with. On the other hand, if you have a good contractor and are looking for an architect, ask the same question of the contractor. The good experiences he has had will be helpful in choosing an architect that will work well with that contractor. This can ferret out a lot of the problems that you otherwise might encounter if you were to just go through it blindly on your own.

Realistic Schedules

It usually takes sixty days for a typical tenant improvement project to be completed. That can, however, run up into twelve weeks. I've seen it take months and months and months. If your contractor is worth his salt, you'll find that he can get the job done in sixty days, assuming that there's nothing overly complicated about your space. Honestly, I've seen people with very complicated spaces have their projects done very quickly. That's something you can use as a guiding rule. Explain to them, "Look, I expect this to be done in sixty days. I expect you to take about sixty days to finish this." Based on that sixty days, you should receive an invoice at the thirty-day mark and then another at the sixty-day mark. That's pretty much industry standard.

What you want to do is actually visit the job site. You should go to the site and look at the work every other day. If you're relying upon a construction manager, he'll be doing the same thing. I also recommend that you have your architect review the project at the point of each payment before you cut a check to the contractor.

When you receive the first invoice, both you and the architect should sign off on the details. The architect needs to sign off on each invoice to reassure you, "Yes, this work has been done." You've got a professional who's looking at the work and understands his plans and is able to judge, "They are saying that they've done about 40 percent of the work. I'm looking at it right now, I've reviewed the site, I've reviewed the work and yes, I agree that they've done that amount of work." The architect then signs off on it, you sign off on it, and you have a record. Then you can issue a payment to your contractor.

> **The architect needs to sign off on each invoice.**

Before You Make That Last Payment

At the end of the project, the contractor will bill you for the remaining portion of the original contract. But you're going to hold back 10 percent.

Why? You must hold back a portion of the final payment if the building inspector hasn't signed the permit cards saying, "Yes, this project is totally completed based on the plans that you submitted to the city. Now you, as a tenant, can occupy the space. This is an occupy-able space now from all perspectives as far as the city is concerned and the fire department and life and safety. Everything has been completed and is satisfactory such that you can go in and operate your business." In the business, this is referred to as having the project "finalled."

Until that occurs, you *definitely* want to hold back 10 percent. That's going to be the carrot in front of the contractor's face that encourages him to do a final push and get everything done. Believe me, inspectors will not final a project if they don't feel it's final. They are very tough. They will do you no favors, and they have got no interest in your success. The inspection for the certificate of occupancy (COO) is the last piece of leverage that they have to make sure that everything gets done the way they want it to be done, the way it *should* be done.

> ◆
> **You *definitely* want to hold back 10 percent.**
> ◆

Unless everything is perfect and exactly how it should be, the inspector will not give you a final on the project. I've watched inspectors go through projects and not give a final on the project because of the color of the screws that were used to mount different electrical gear. Until those screws were replaced with the right color screws (indicating certain elements of the electrical system), they were not going to finalize the building. They certainly weren't going to sit around and wait for you to do it while they're standing there that day. You're going to have to have them come back and re-inspect your project once you've done what they've asked you to do.

As I've said, inspectors can be very tough. Even if the contractor is working as hard as he can, until he satisfies the inspector he's not going to get that final. If he doesn't get the final, the space is worth as much to you as before they'd even snapped the lines to lay out your suite. If you can't operate your business in the suite, it doesn't matter what progress has been made. The bottom line is this: you can't operate your business in the suite. Finalling the permit is the only possible way.

You're also going to want to hold back 10 percent until you've done what is called in the industry, "the walkthrough." The walkthrough is done when the suite has been completed, the work has been finalled, and all the finishes are in. Now, you're going to walk through the suite with the architect and check *everything*. You're going to check the outlets, you're going to check the miniblinds, and you're going to check the doors.

One of the biggest things you're going to check is the walls. Make sure the nicks are fixed, and the paint colors are right. You must also check that the flooring is done correctly, and that there's not something wrong with it such as a scratch, a tear, or stain. Check that the ceilings are done correctly, that there are no broken ceiling tiles, for instance. If there are, it may not be the fault of the contractor. For example, if the timing is not properly planned, the guys that you hired to do your data and phone wiring may have come in after the ceiling was installed. They'll have to go through it and will most likely break ceiling tiles. Sometimes a contractor is willing to replace a few broken ceiling tiles caused by someone else, but it is not their responsibility.

This brings up an important point. If you have a subcontractor that you hire to do work outside of your tenant improvement contractor's scope, such as phone wiring or alarm system, you are responsible for the work that your subcontractor provides and any damage he causes to the site. You should expect your TI contractor to be willing to monitor and coordinate with your subcontractor, but monitoring and coordinating is different than being responsible for their work. If your subcontractor delays the project or causes damage to the project, like ceiling tiles or drywall, it is *not* reasonable to hold that against your contractor.

The walkthrough can take several hours, so plan accordingly. Do not rush. Take your time; and as you go, mark everything that needs attention and have your contractor *write everything down—most often the contractor will create the list*. Take a digital camera and take pictures as part of your documentation. Go from room to room to room, methodically. Have each room numbered so there is no confusion later; in most architectural space plans they number the rooms for reference. For example, make note

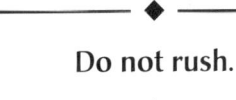

Do not rush.

that in Room 101 there were nicks in the wall; describe *where* they are and be specific. The contractor will distribute this list to the architect, you, and his relevant subcontractors. The contractor will have these subcontractors come out, and based on the list will make the repairs and corrections. Usually, this kind of thing shouldn't take more than a week unless it's something that was a major screw up on the project— say, they put in the wrong toilet, or the sink is in the wrong place, or the light fixtures are wrong. That's when it may take longer, especially if they have to order a part. You can see why you'll want to wait until that walkthrough has been done before you make your final payment.

There's an additional strategy I recommend as well. Try to design an agreement with your contractor that allows you to operate your practice for thirty days before your final payment. That arrangement is ideal for you. It's generally not something that a contractor is going to agree to, but you can always ask. If you can get your contractor to agree to it, it's greatly to your advantage. Keep in mind: it may not be necessary as most tenant improvements come with a one-year warranty.

The Details of Your Payment Terms

During negotiations with your contractor regarding payment— which will include discussion of your holding back 10 percent at the end, what the conditions are for that payment to be made, and so on—you will ask your contractor to sign what's called a "conditional lien release" *before* making your first payment. The conditional lien release says, "Once I cash this check, and it clears, I will waive my right to put a lien on your property."

The reason this is important is that you don't want to have your contractor lien the developer's or the landlord's property. Often, at least in all the leases I write, if your contractor liens the property, you're now in default. You really want to avoid that. It can become a very nasty legal situation and can cost lots of money. A conditional lien release is a great way to avoid that.

After you've reached that agreement with your contractor, when you receive his next progress invoice, have him sign an "unconditional lien release" waiver for the prior payment he received. That first time, he signed a *conditional lien release* waiver. Now he's going to sign an *unconditional lien release* waiver for that previous amount paid. He's going to waive that whole amount of the last check. You'll continue this process until you've completed all payments, first a conditional lien release, then an unconditional lien release. I would strongly recommend that you do not pay your contractor until he has signed the conditional lien releases and the unconditional lien releases at the appropriate times.

> You'll continue this process until you've completed all payments, first a conditional lien release, then an unconditional lien release.

A Deal Breaker

The contractor signing these waivers should be a deal killer for you. Contractors don't like to lose those rights. They want to have as many rights as they can keep. If they lose their ability to lien the property, they lose some of the leverage they have against you. They're not going to want to do that. A professional contractor, however, understands and has done this many times and will readily sign it; he understands that that's just part of doing business. Be assured that this is certainly not an unusual request. Don't feel awkward for asking for it. You simply will not pay, period, unless contractors have signed these waivers. I do not do business with a contractor who won't agree to this.

Bidding—The Architect's Role

Because of the complications of the bidding process and the major coordination that goes into dealing with all the plans, the architect should be the one handling the bids. As I mentioned before, the architect's role should be one where he is the hub of the project, that he is controlling the entire project through the drawings, through the city and, ultimately, through the construction. He should also be handling the bidding. He's the one who's intimately aware of his plans and is, therefore, the one best able to answer any questions that come up during the bidding process.

This would include the engineer's drawings. The architect will have to coordinate the engineer's drawings, which will include the mechanical, electrical and plumbing (MEP), with his drawings and become familiar with the details of the MEP drawings to ensure there are no conflicts between them. Once again, being the point person, he is the best one for the contractor to ask for clarifications of the engineering drawings unless it's something overly technical that the architect needs to pass the question back to the engineers.

> **The more contractors looking at the plans, the more likely that someone will point out things that might otherwise have been missed.**

It's the architect's responsibility to get a set of construction drawings to each contractor chosen to be considered in the bidding process. Typically the contractor will make copies to send to his subcontractor, but there are times when a contractor will ask the architect to make copies. You're going to want to have at least three contractors in the bidding process. That's going to give you a high, middle, and low. You can have up to five if you want, and that's something that I recommend.

One of the benefits of having more contractors looking at the plans is simply that you have more eyes on the plans. That's going to lead to more questions and clarifications of the drawings. As result, the drawings are going to become better. The architect is going to realize that there are some areas that are consistently getting questions and they need clarification.

The more contractors looking at the plans, the more likely that someone will point out things that might otherwise have been missed. Doing so allows you to have the most complete set of plans. When a contractor points out something that just doesn't make sense and ultimately may not work, the architect is forced to go back and look at his drawings. He may need to change a thing or two, or at least note the issue so that during the construction phase he can adjust his drawings accordingly.

While you're going to want to have at least three contractors bidding on the process, you're also going to want to have at least three subcontractors per major trade. Major trades are plumbing, HVAC, electrical, and framing. If there will be any "specialty" construction occurring in the suite, to accommodate items like linear accelerators, CT scanners, or technical suites like sleep centers, you'll want to have three subcontractors on that as well.

You definitely want to clearly communicate to the contractors bidding out your improvement that you expect them not to use any "greensheet" subcontractors. A greensheet subcontractor is someone that the contractors have never used before. Contractors have a list of subcontractors in the area they can reference. If the contractor has never worked in the area or wants to try a new subcontractor for a particular trade, he can use this list. The problem is there is no history of performance or quality of work.

You want to have somebody that the contractor has used before. You want to make sure that they work well together and, more importantly, that, the contractor is aware of the quality of work that the subcontractor does, including the subcontractor's ability to perform on time, which can often be a big problem.

A lot of times, subcontractors can overbook or not have reliable workers. You need to know, as a doctor, that your suite is going to be done on time. If the contractor has never used the subcontractor before, he's not going to be able to vouch for the timeliness and the quality of the subcontractor's work. You don't want that type of situation. You want to make sure that it's clear to all contractors bidding on your project that you expect them to have experience with any subcontractor they engage.

Details of Bids

It is important that you communicate to each contractor clearly what you expect the bid to look like. If you don't describe, in detail, what you expect from them, the contractors will give you the easiest bid they can produce. For some, that would be a single sheet of paper with some very general information—maybe plumbing, electrical, HVAC, framing, flooring, and so forth, broken out in general terms. They won't indicate, for example, the number of linear square feet for the millwork, or the number of faucets, or light fixtures, etc. You're left looking at these general numbers to try and understand exactly what is included and excluded in their bid. That becomes problematic later when you review the various bids. Make sure you communicate that you want an itemized list with each individual element priced on each item.

Additionally, you're going to want to give them a timetable. What I've found with most contractors, even when they're really busy, is that they can produce a bid within a week. That gives them time to get the plans to the subcontractors and allows those subcontractors enough time to look at the plans, ask any questions they may have, and get the bids back. The contractors then take a day to compile all the bids, put them in a format that's acceptable to you, and return them to the architect.

Initially, what you'll most often receive from the contractor is the itemized list you requested. What they typically won't do is give you a breakout of what each subcontractor provided to them. They'll generally give you the one that they believe is going to perform the best or that gives you the best price. *Make sure that you ask to see the supporting bids.* Each subcontractor will fax in the bid for their particular trade. You can request that you see these to substantiate the bids that you received from your contractors, and I recommend that you do that. Although it is time consuming, keep this information on file so that you can reference it at a later time if you should need to while you're going through the bid review.

I also suggest for that you request that the contractors provide recommendations they feel would save you money. This is often referred to as "value engineering." What you're looking for is an alternative, suggestions from the contractor or subcontractor, for materials that perform the same function or look the same but are valued at a lower price than the item or method that the architect has proposed. This can be very valuable to you when you can see how well the contractor and his subs are thinking, how creative they are, how versed they are in the type of construction you're looking for them to do. And, you can get some ideas or products suggested to you that even the architect may not be familiar with.

Because your architect isn't a specialist in each trade, he will need to rely upon each of the trades to make suggestions for less expensive alternatives to his specifications. I've often seen tens of thousands of dollars being saved through this process, so this is something that I would highly recommend you ask for. Ultimately, once you do pick your contractor, go back again and ask them to check for alternatives again. You'll often find that when the contractor knows he's got the job, he's even more willing to make such suggestions (which he may not have wanted to share until he knew that you were going to hire him).

Now you're familiar with the process of getting the plans out, answering the questions, and getting the numbers back. You've got three to five contractors' bids. It's time for the architect to roll up his sleeves and make sure that each of the submitted bids is comparable to each other, otherwise called making sure it's "apples to apples." What you're really trying to do is find out which bid is the most cost effective, meets the timeline you've requested, and provides a high quality of work.

If you have a contractor who is suggesting 400 square feet of something and another contractor who measured out 200 square feet of something, you're not going to catch that discrepancy unless you make sure that they call those out in detailed bids. You want bids to list the linear feet of the walls, countertops, and cabinets.

For each detail cited in a bid, you want the quantity given as well, whether it is in the measuring form of distance or number.

For example, if there are supposed to be fourteen sinks in your suite, make sure each contractor has called out fourteen sinks in his bid. If you notice that one contractor has called out nine and his price is lower, you will know that contractor didn't catch all of the sinks planned for your suite, and you should wonder what other details he has missed. This is important because you want to make sure you use a contractor who is skilled in his analysis of the drawings. If the contractor's subcontractors can't catch these things and do it accurately upfront, that should tell you that you're probably going to have some issues with them during the construction. You want a detail-oriented contractor and you want him hiring detail-oriented subcontractors.

This step in examining bids is an excellent way to make sure that you're going to get a contractor who pays attention to details. If they are missing things during the bidding process, they're probably not the person that you want to use. You should be able to avoid this by relying on the architect's experience to include for consideration only the contractors with whom he or she has worked.

I shouldn't need to discuss this last part, but I must say something because I've seen people accept hourly contracts as opposed to a "fixed contract." It is imperative that you know up front the costs that you will incur during construction. It is *not* reasonable for the contractor to ask you for an hourly contract. If a contractor is asking you for an hourly contract, I can assure you this is someone who is not a professional. This is not someone you should hire.

> **It is *not* reasonable for the contractor to ask you for an hourly contract.**

As I've said, you should be able to avoid this kind of contractor by relying on your architect. But there are instances where a contractor, who in the past, did fixed contracts, decides to change the way he does things and is now issuing a "time and materials-based" contract. That is definitely not something you want. It may not necessarily be the fault of the architect; if he hasn't used the contractor in a year, he wouldn't be aware of this change, but it is his responsibility to catch that stuff both during and after the bidding process.

Turn-Key

There's also what's called a "turn-key" process. This is when *you* don't have to do anything. You just tell the developer, "I want you to handle everything. I want you to do the build-out. I want you to handle the design. I want you to handle the city. I want you to pay for everything." There are reasons why developers might agree to this. It may be that the market is demanding it and the developer needs to remain competitive. It may be that he wants to set himself apart from his competition by offering turn-key build-outs. Often, it's very time consuming to manage construction, handle the design, and coordinate with all the consultants. Offering to take that load can be very appealing to many doctors. After all, you're trying to run your practice. You're not a real estate professional. You really want to focus on what you have been highly trained to do, and that's take care of your patients.

> A turn-key deal will involve the developer hiring the architect, hiring the contractor, coordinating everybody and running the project.

What does a turn-key look like? Generally, a turn-key deal will involve the developer hiring the architect, hiring the contractor, coordinating everybody and running the project. Your involvement will be solely in making decisions that are relevant to you. While you may feel that everything is relevant to you, you'll find that, really, you just need to ensure that the space plan is correct.

Of course, you're going to need to decide the finishes, such as carpet, paint colors, wall coverings, window treatments, type of cabinets, and any other design elements that are relevant to the work you do or the way that you want your office to look. As time consuming as these decisions can be, they are nothing compared to the work the developer is taking on for you in a turn-key situation.

During the construction phase, you'll be looking at the construction, making sure it's what you envisioned and wanted. Quite often, you'll realize that you really need an outlet "there" or you want an additional light "here." Some of these things can be easily accommodated during construction, although generally it's more expensive to do it that way. That's why I highly recommend that you figure all those details out during the drawing phase, when it's just a matter of moving a line as opposed to moving an outlet.

> ◆
>
> A good developer who cares about your practice will insist they perform disruptive work only during non-business hours.
>
> ◆

Of course, because the design is reliant upon your wishes, it could conceivably cost a lot more money than the developer has budgeted when he planned the building. Quite often, what you'll find as part of a turn-key agreement is a cap on the expenses. That is typically communicated in the form of a price per square foot; the developer agrees to a turn-key plan as long as it doesn't exceed a certain amount of dollars per square foot.

If you have a 1,000-square foot suite and the developer doesn't want to spend more than $20,000 on your suite for design and construction, including the permits and plan checks, he will communicate that he will do a turn-key build out based on $20 a foot. Anything over that will be an additional charge, which you would be required to cover.

This means that although you're responsible for the choices you make in a turn-key, as long as you keep them reasonable, you shouldn't have to come up with payments beyond the cap the developer has suggested, provided the developer is knowledgeable in what it takes to build a standard medical suite.

So, you have choices. You can manage the entire process of the design and construction, or have a developer take care of the whole thing for you, or land somewhere between these two scenarios. If you decide to have a developer handle the job, look for one who's been in the business for a long time. This will ensure you are working with someone who really cares about the properties he produces, the tenants who are in them, and the relationships that are developed.

A professional and qualified developer will review the plans, whether he is in charge of them or not, to make sure that they coincide properly with the construction of the building; for instance, you don't want to have walls that end in windows, which can be unsightly form the outside, or other problems of that nature. In addition, he will review the construction as it progresses. Often, I've found that going out to the site at least once a week to review what the tenant improvement contractor is doing is an important element to protect the building.

Often, they'll make penetrations in the roof that weren't on the plans. These need to be handled by the roofing contractor who installed the roof in order to maintain his warranty. Issues like this frequently arise during the construction phase of the project. Someone on site, who is looking out for the interests of the building, should be particularly important to you. You don't want a tenant-improvement contractor damaging the main sewer line, or the water lines, or electrical equipment, and thereby affecting the other tenants in the building.

There are often existing tenants in the building, already operating their businesses, in which you plan to have your suite. A professional developer will be protective of those tenants and require that the tenant-improvement contractor not perform any noisy construction during business hours. This kind of requirement needs to be communicated to the contractor prior to signing a contract. This kind of scheduling may mean that he will have to pay the subcontractors more than he would otherwise because they will be working at times that are not normal business hours, such as late in the evening or even overnight.

Frequently, contractors like to start their day at about six in the morning. They can use those early hours before most offices are open, which is usually between eight and nine, to do noisy work. If they think the noise is going to continue longer than that, they need to plan accordingly. A good developer, who cares about your practice, will insist they only perform disruptive work only during non-business hours. You'll appreciate your developer's attention to matters like this once you're in your suite, sharing the building with the other tenants. You can start off with on a good foot with your new neighbors if they have not been inconvenienced by the construction of your suite.

While the construction phase of tenant improvements can be the most intimidating part of the process, it actually is the least time consuming for you. You'll find that you will spend most of your time on the design of your suite and working with the architect to make sure the plans are exactly what you want. If you do that hard work up front, the construction phase will go very easily, provided that you have an architect who is experienced with medical property and with getting things approved through the city.

Inspections

Bear in mind that the city and the city's inspectors are going to make sure everything is up to code. You can rely on them, knowing they work hard to do their job and that they don't do favors for contractors. You'll find that inspectors are diligent and professional, although at times a bit individualistic, not caring necessarily that the plan-check process didn't catch something. That type of problem is irrelevant to them. What they care about is that it's built the way that they think it should be built according to their interpretation of the code. At the end of the day, they will always win. The plan-check department will always lose that battle.

Unless there's a compelling reason or it's an overwhelming financial burden, it is generally not productive to argue and fight with the inspector. A word of advice: when dealing with the inspectors, respect is important. They understand that they are the ones that have to approve your build-out; otherwise you're not going to be able to occupy your suite. Because they are aware of their power, they often will use it. If you make the mistake of upsetting the inspector at the beginning of the process, you'll find that he can make the entire construction process very difficult for you. He can do that by making sure the most conservative interpretation of the code is adhered to, making it more expensive and time consuming for you.

And, honestly, at the end of the day, there'll be nothing you can do about it. If you have a good contractor, though, this shouldn't be an issue. If you *do* feel that you need to get involved in the process because a contractor is telling you that the city or the inspector is seemingly overly critical or not performing as expected by not returning plan checks on time or coming out to the site as scheduled, call the architect. See if the architect, who has developed a relationship with the city, can ease their concerns. That said, I've observed that often the owner has more clout. There may be a time when you may have to get involved as the owner of the suite. For whatever reason, the city and governmental agencies will be more responsive to what you have to say, even if you say the exact same thing that your consultants say.

> ◆
> **I've observed that often the owner has more clout.**
> ◆

Your construction process should go well if you've done your homework in the beginning by

1. Finding a good architect
2. Finding a good contractor
3. Making a good set of plans

You'll find that the construction phase is actually quite an exciting time because you get to see your vision take shape in real life.

THINGS *to* REMEMBER

1. Watch out for the contractor that bids low and then issues change orders once he gets the contract.

2. Require itemized and detailed bids.

3. Do not pay upfront; instead make progress payments.

4. Hold back 10 percent until the walk-through repairs are completed.

5. Require unconditional lien releases.

Chapter Six
OPERATING YOUR BUSINESS

The fact that you're reading this book tells me you are planning on operating your own private practice. If this is your first practice, congratulations! Running your own business can be one of the most profound experiences you will have. While it is not something that you think about as you go through medical school—where your primary goal is to learn how to care for your patients—now that you've chosen to open your own practice, it will be important for you to be a successful businessperson.

There are many books that can teach you how to be a successful businessperson, and there are many consultants who can help as you strive to accomplish your dream of running your own practice. Although I'm not going to get into every detail, I do have something to share on the topic that I believe will be instrumental to your success.

Employees

Once you grasp the fundamentals of how to run a business, there are some other essentials, often overlooked that will help your business succeed without any real additional effort.

Taking care of your employees is at the top of the list. Your employees will, in many ways, interact with your patients more than you will and will often be your hands and feet over the course of your practice's life. Choosing your employees wisely and treating them well is an important element of creating a practice that people will want to visit. You will retain your patients longer and they will generally feel more satisfied with the service they receive if you have happy employees.

> Choosing your employees wisely and treating them well is an important element of creating a practice that people will want to visit.

There is nothing quite as disappointing as interacting with a hostile employee who doesn't understand the importance of making a patient feel welcome, at home, and comfortable, that they are been taking care of with genuine concern. Frequently employees will feel stressed because of the pressure from the type of high-volume operation so common in the United States. Regardless of why they feel this way, it often correlates with how they are treated by you and how they treat your patients.

When you treat your employees with respect, compassion, and dignity, you honor their role and the value they bring to your practice. The employees will in turn respect, honor, and show compassion to your patients.

An excellent way of "taking care" of your employees is to use incentives. The reason I like incentivizing employees is that it gives them ownership in the task they are performing. While ideally they should do everything with their whole hearts simply for the love of it, that isn't a realistic expectation to have of your employees. There are many ways you can incentivize your employees, and patient retention is an excellent way to motivate them. Give them a goal of achieving a certain patient retention number, and tell them that they will receive a bonus at the end of the year if they have been able to maintain that level of patient retention. By giving them this incentive, your staff will view every interaction with a patient as an opportunity to retain them.

Also, think about the incentive of keeping appointments on time. When staff is scheduling patients, they should consider the way that you work and schedule appropriately. This will cause them to look at each of the visits as they bring the patient in, take their vitals, and make sure that everything is on schedule. Ideally, all the vitals will have been taken, and you will have been given the chart and the time to review it prior to you walking into the exam room.

Billing is also an excellent area to incentivize your employees. How quickly they file the paperwork, the way they turn things around for an insurance companies, the way they interact with patients to collect the necessary information for billing, and the accuracy of their coding can all play an important part in the financial success of your practice.

> **When you treat your employees with respect, compassion, and dignity, you honor their role and the value they bring to your practice.**

However you choose to incentivize them, do it in a way that motivates them to act with the behavior you seek. Make sure that the method of incentivizing does not contribute to poor behavior, and believe me, there are incentives that can cause a response that's opposite to the one you want.

An excellent example of the way that an incentive program can go wrong can be seen in the way some hospitals profit share with their doctors. While this idea in and of itself is not a bad one, it certainly can lead to potential problems if taken in the wrong direction. For example, when doctor groups are incentivized by profit sharing, they have the potential to make decisions that are profitable for the hospital but cause a negative experience for the patient being treated. This is clearly not the goal of the hospital or the doctors, but brings to light the necessity of looking at the incentive you provide and then analyzing how the incentive is affecting your business.

Track Your Progress

It is important to track all aspects of your practice. Track how long the patient was in your office, from the moment the patient walked in the door to the moment the patient left your office. Keep logs of how long it took you to completely provide the service to your patient. But don't stop there. Look at these logs, and look at the trends that appear. If you notice that a certain type of patient is taking longer in your office, your staff should schedule accordingly so you are not making other patients wait while you deal with the lengthy visit a particular patient requires.

Also track how long it takes you to be paid by the insurance companies, and analyze your business to see if there are ways you can expedite the process. This will be the only way you can truly know how efficiently your office is running. If you decide to run a practice based on insurance payments and contract with the insurance companies that provide you the patients, it is essential that you track all elements of your business that are relative to making a profit.

Whether you decide to incentivize your employees, you should still keep in mind that your employees, no matter how dedicated they appear, are there to work and be paid.

Consider allowing your employees to receive a share of the profits when they reach a certain level of seniority. It is an excellent way to involve them in the process, and will help to create a more entrepreneurial spirit. Even at the lower levels of your practice, they don't have to be partners in order to enjoy the thrilling feeling of contributing to a successful business.

Give your employees a voice.

When your staff feels that they have a voice in the company, they will be more willing to vocalize their thoughts and suggestions, and you'll be pleasantly surprised at the ideas they come up with. When they feel you don't care or that you're not open to their suggestions, they will often feel disrespected and dishonored. So give your employees a voice. Allow them to have times to meet with you and share ideas they think could contribute to a more successful practice. If they know you are willing to listen to their ideas, they will continue to share them throughout their tenure with you. And it is important to remember: they are the ones intimately involved with the work you have assigned to them. If you have picked exceptional people, remember the qualities that originally drew you to them. You need to trust that these qualities are going to enable them to contribute to your practice.

One of the ways this process can be more productive is when you let staff know of your vision, in writing. It's important that you have a strong vision of what your practice is to be, how you want to treat your patients, how you want to treat your employees, and how you want your practice to contribute to the community.

> You need to have your vision firmly seated in your heart.

You need to have your vision firmly seated in your heart. By focusing steadily upon your vision and trusting that it's a good one, you will be taking a great step toward overcoming the obstacles that you will undoubtedly encounter as your practice grows.

You may need to change your vision as your practice grows, and you become more experienced and develop a greater understanding of the path you want to take. But the overall theme shouldn't vary, and you should remain steadfast in pursuing your vision as something you firmly believe in and intend on fully living out. This is why you should share your vision with your partners, your associates, and your employees.

By giving your partners, associates, and employees the opportunity to participate in your vision, you provide a context in which the suggestions they make will be more applicable. Have meetings, issue memos, and schedule times when you all get together. Continue to present your vision and continue to instill that vision in your partners, associates, and employees. In this way, your vision will become theirs and the values you want to bring to your partners, employees, patients, and community will be brought to all of them.

Often, as we get busy, we forget that even the smallest of compliments can encourage our co-workers as they struggle through their day. You'll have your own troubles and stresses from your personal life as well as your professional life that you'll bring to work. Recognizing the efforts each person makes and acknowledging the accomplishments of each other will go a long way toward encouraging those around you to stay the course. If you do this, your employees will find happiness at their workplace, and your patients will be grateful for your practice.

> ◆ **Continue to present your vision and continue to instill that vision in your partners, associates, and employees.** ◆

You should, of course, also give your patients a voice. If you're running a high-volume practice, your patients are aware that your time is very valuable. They will get the message that they won't get a lot of time with you. But you can make most of those feelings go away by taking just a few seconds at the end of each patient visit to ask a few questions.

Ask if you have covered everything that they were concerned about. Ask if there is anything else they would like to speak with you about. Ask them how their experience was with the front desk, or how difficult it was for them to schedule an appointment. Did they have a long wait?

> ◆ **Also give your patients a voice.** ◆

Don't be afraid of the answers—what you learn will help you to develop better ways of running your office. When you take a few minutes to ask these questions, your patients will feel as though they also have a voice and are participating in the success of your practice.

Finally, the only way I've found to truly make a mark is when I go in the opposite direction that everyone else is heading. This is something you should consider as you develop your vision. Do you want to do what everyone else has already done and is doing, or would you prefer to bring something new to the community? If you prefer to be innovative, or if there is a high level of competition in your area, you will need to consider how to provide a service that others in your area don't. Again, have your employees share with you how they believe things could be improved. Look at what your peers are doing and figure out how you can improve on it. The choices you make and the value your practice brings to the community will ultimately have a great affect on the success or failure of your practice.

Even though we are in an age that tells us to promote ourselves, to boost ourselves up, to make others around us think highly of us, there is nothing better for your practice and your patients than to put yourself last. When it comes to running your practice, you should always think of yourself last and put everything else first.

> **There is nothing better for your practice and your patients than to put yourself last.**

Of course, the patient should be the primary "first" on your list, the first of all firsts. The patient is the reason you have your practice, the patient is the reason you studied and worked for all those years receiving nearly no pay. Don't lose sight of the patient when you open your practice.

Yes, the financial burdens you carry from starting your practice as well as your school loans can be terrifying. You're going to be motivated to take that pressure away and you *should* be motivated to do that, but not at the expense of the patient.

The Right Employees

As I have already mentioned, the employees are the heart of your practice. You need to take care of your employees. But you first need to pick the right employees.

Hiring the right employees is critical to the success of your practice. How do you find employees? It might be tempting to put an ad in the local newspaper or to use the Internet, but after talking to some of the top doctors in southern California, I recommend that you use an employment agency.

This entails a greater expense, initially, than an ad in the newspaper and on the Internet. But the money you would save using the newspaper or the Internet will be quickly offset by the time you'll spend filtering through all the applications. Ask yourself whether that is time worth spending, or whether your time is better spent on other work. With an employment agency, you remove the task of sorting through all the multitude of applications and applicants.

An employment agency will be able to draw upon its resources to find just the right person for you. They will interview the candidates prior to you interviewing them and, if you've communicated well with them and they've listened well to you, they should have a strong sense of the type of employee you are looking for. I do not recommend using a medical specialty employment agency, at least not for your front office staff. You are far better off looking for someone who is interested in getting into the medical field and working in a medical office, but who doesn't have any experience because you can train that person to be the type of employee you need. What it comes down to is personality and attitude, not skill base and knowledge. You can give your staff the skills and knowledge. Over time, their skills and knowledge will increase as they learn and develop as an employee. Look for someone who is trainable more than someone who is knowledgeable. Ideally, you want both. But if you have to pick, pick trainable.

So, let's say you have chosen an employment agency. They have found some great potential employees. They call you and want to schedule some interviews, but maybe you've never interviewed anyone before. Maybe you have no idea how to run an interview. The employment agency can help you with that by supplying you some of the questions that, in their experience, are important. There will be the obvious questions, ones that you will, most likely, have been asked yourself when you applied for a job prior to school, or even during school. Those basic questions are easy to come up with and they will give you some information on the type of person you have sitting in front of you, but I would like to suggest that you change your perspective a bit.

Don't run the interview from the perspective of a doctor hiring an employee, but rather take the perspective of the patient. How would a patient feel interacting with this person? What does their attitude say to you from a patient's perspective? Does his or her personality make you feel comfortable? Ask yourself these questions and write down your observations as you interview the potential employee.

You may find it helpful to have another person at the interview, either observing the applicant as you are talking with them or asking the questions while you observe and get a feeling for how you would, as a patient, feel hearing the way this applicant talks and expresses herself. Don't discount your intuition as you interview the applicant. Often, what you are picking up on are the signals from their body language. Be sensitive to the feelings you have during the interview. These feelings can give you insights you may not otherwise get and can help you decide whether to choose one applicant over another.

While hiring may seem a difficult task, firing someone is far more difficult. Keep in mind: a person can be developed and trained as they work for you and learn how to do their job. But as Dr. Kenneth Tokita, of the Cancer Center of Irvine, told me several times as we talked about this topic: "You can't change a person's attitude!"

> **While hiring may seem a difficult task, firing someone is far more difficult.**

If someone has a bad attitude it is important you fire them as soon as possible. If you don't fire them, the harmony that you have strived to develop in your practice will slowly dissipate as the bad attitude of your employee spreads throughout the office.

Another important reason to fire someone or a group of people is if cliques develop in your office. Cliques should be considered one of the most destructive things that can occur in your office. This comment may seem strange when you first hear it. But when you think about what cliques do, I think you'll agree. When a clique forms, it means that other people are being excluded; immediately, harmonies in your office are broken. This disharmony will play itself out through all interactions—with the patients and other staff as well as with you. One group will be disinclined to help another group, and your team will lose the connectedness you so strongly want and need. Your patients will sense the disharmony, which will make them uncomfortable and more likely to switch to another provider.

If you see a clique form, you must address it immediately, and if it isn't corrected by the people in it, Dr. Tokita recommends that you fire *everyone* in the clique. This act sends a clear message to the rest of your employees that cliques will not be tolerated, that excluding other people will not be tolerated. It will clearly communicate that you insist upon everyone helping one another and in treating everyone as though they were their brother or their sister.

Whatever the reason for firing someone, I can assure you that if you have come to the point where you realize you need to do it, your patients and employees (as well as the person you're firing) will benefit from your decision. First, you'll be benefiting your patients because they will no longer have to interact with an employee who does not represent your standard of excellence. As you recall, I made it clear that your patient must be the number one priority in your practice. You must be willing to take the necessary steps to ensure that your patient is receiving the absolute best care they can receive. These concepts are simply the golden rule of "treating others as you would want to be treated." But more important than that is the idea that you need to treat others how they want to be treated. Taking care of your patients by getting rid of people that don't treat them well is essential to maintaining a high level of customer service and achieving patient retention.

Your employees will also benefit. When you fire bad employees, your other employees see that you have a standard that is clearly communicated, expected, and enforced.

Keep in mind that your employees are watching to see what you do about a bad employee who is not keeping up with the standards that you have laid forth in your vision for your company.

When I first started learning how to train my nine-week-old golden retriever, I wanted to know the best way to train him, the most effective way I could teach him to behave in the way that I desired. After much research and trial and error I found that there are three key elements to successfully dealing with an unacceptable behavior. As silly as it may sound, I found these three key elements to be true in raising my children. The three elements I find to be essential are consistency, motivation, and timing.

> **The three elements I find to be essential are consistency, motivation, and timing.**

When you are dealing with a situation that is unacceptable in your practice, you must first and foremost be consistent. As parents, we all struggle with consistency and we all fail at times. Still, you must focus on being consistent with your level of standards; otherwise, people will see that you arbitrarily enforce your expectations. A sense of unfairness will creep into their view of how you run your practice, and they will talk about you amongst themselves.

You must be consistent with every issue that comes up. If a behavior deviates from the standards and expectations you've communicated clearly to your employees, deal with it every time.

Secondly, deal with it in such a way that motivates the person and the others in the group to take the discipline to heart. If one of your employees stole $100,000 from your business, for example, even if you address it immediately but tell her that her punishment will be coming in fifteen minutes early for the next week, it is not going to motivate your other employees (or the employee that stole the $100,000) to recognize that you mean business when you say that stealing will not be tolerated. Clearly, if you are in this situation you are going to have to find a better way of motivating your employees!

Finally, the timing should be immediate and decisive. Don't let time pass; once you learn of the infraction, address the issue immediately.

Understand that one of the ways you will have to deal with an infraction is to fire the individual. You will not only help your patients and employees by doing this, but also the person you're firing—you will teach them that there are people in life who mean what they say. Usually, the person you're firing hasn't met many people like you, but I can assure you if they do meet enough people like you, they'll be far more likely to change the way they do things.

You can greatly help people by holding them to high standards and enforcing them. Some of the best ways that we learn us as human beings is through failure. We tend not to learn nearly as much through our successes. Keep that in mind when you fire someone. In many ways, you're helping them to become a better person. Whether they look at that as an opportunity to become a better person and actually take steps to become a better person is not your problem. Regardless, you are creating the opportunity for them to become a better person and if you're like most people who run businesses, you more than likely have given them several opportunities to improve and develop long before firing them. So don't let your conscience bother you if you come to the point where you realize that you need to let someone go.

> ◆
> **You can greatly help people by holding them to high standards and enforcing them.**
> ◆

While I was studying police gunfights and reading stories and governmental analysis of gunfights that have been documented time and again, it was clearly demonstrated that the officer chose to finally use deadly force long after they legally had the right to exert that deadly force in the situation. What can we take away from this as human beings, who are normally socialized and conditioned? We will opt to go out of our way to give people opportunities to make corrections prior to executing a decisive and final consequence on the person. Both terminating someone's life and terminating someone's job will most likely occur, research has shown, long after it should have occurred. It should not be your concern about whether the person can support themselves financially or whether they can work for someone else.

Your sole focus should be to provide for your patients. So I would encourage you to not feel guilty if you have to let someone go, but rather look at it as an opportunity to allow them to learn (if they choose to take it that way), and ultimately move forward in their life.

So, who should you hire when you are first opening your practice and in what order should you hire people? During your first six months of operations, your front desk person and your billing person are really the only two people you will need to operate your practice. It is some doctors' opinions that these two people will be more important than a nurse while your practice is in its infancy stage.

Your front desk person will be the heart and soul of your practice. When you walk into a hotel and want to know where to go in the city, what to do, or what to expect, the person who handles all this is a concierge. They will suggest restaurants based on your preferences; they will have an intimate knowledge of the area and be able to recommend different leisure activities. In other words, they will take care of you from the moment you walk into the hotel up to the moment you leave.

Your front desk person should consider herself a concierge. It will be her responsibility to provide an excellent and an overwhelmingly positive experience to each of your patients from the moment they walk in the door to the moment they walk out. She should be thoroughly concerned with the welfare of the patient, the comfort of the patient, and should be willing to address any of the patient's questions or concerns while they are in your office.

Another way to think of the front desk's responsibility is to think of a caretaker. This must be someone who is nurturing; someone who is "motherly" is an excellent choice for this position.

Likewise, a good billing person will be critical to your practice. While the billing person's primary job will be to bill the insurance companies and the front desk's primary job should be to tend to your patients, both should be able to interact with them positively, answer the phones, check out your patients, and coordinate the paperwork your patients need to fill out as they enter the suite.

Both should be able to schedule, and both should be able to handle basic billing. You will need them to be interchangeable and able to handle the basic level elements of each job. This will not only ensure that one can cover for another in everyday interactions, but also if one employee is out sick, the other employee should be familiar enough with the employee's obligations that your entire office won't shut down. For the first six months, these two employees should be enough to run your practice. An additional benefit to having just two employees handling your entire front office is that it gives them the ability to understand how everything functions within an office.

As your practice grows, your first two employees will understand how they can help new people who are doing the jobs they once did because, having done them before, they know what that task requires.

The things your original staff members know will benefit the new hires as they learn their jobs and take over more and more of the work the front desk and the billing person were originally doing. When you first start your practice, not only does this help your employees, it will also be more helpful to the patient. A well-rounded employee that understands all the elements of your practice will be able to answer questions that the patient may have, whether they be insurance, scheduling, or any other issues. This will make the patient feel more comfortable interacting with your office.

> **A well-rounded employee that understands all the elements of your practice will be able to answer questions that the patient may have.**

An excellent example of this can be seen in how a shell building is designed and constructed. When we initially design a building, there are many people—sometimes ten to twenty individuals—involved with the design process. Each of these people has a specific task they must understand and execute, whether it is an electrical engineer, a mechanical engineer, and so on. There is also the architect, and the draftsman who handles the drafting of the drawings as they're being designed, the city that the plans are ultimately submitted to, the contractor who will be bidding on the plans, and all of his subcontractors.

You can imagine what confusion would arise if there were no central person to handle all the questions. The people who need answers would be lucky if they received them. The people who need to get the questions would be lucky to hear them. And it would most likely be a miracle if the project actually was completed and approved by the city.

Instead, we structure our projects, particularly in the design phase, so all questions, all answers, and all documents as well as all drawings run through a single point person in our architectural firm. This project manager will handle all communication in the form of a verbal, written, or drawn form.

You can see how much better the process goes when everything runs through one person. Everyone knows who to go to with questions and everyone knows who go to when they want to learn the answer to a question that may have been asked. No one wonders who to call if they need to coordinate something, or if they need more information.

When the plans are finally submitted to the city, which involves an entirely different organization and another whole group of people, the architect will manage the drawings as they go through the city. This is required to get approval from planning, the traffic department, the engineering department, plumbing, mechanical, and electrical—all the different departments are coordinated by a single point person on the city side. While we may have thirty to sixty people involved in the overall design and plan check and permit process, it is all being filtered through a few individuals in a highly organized and successful way.

We have followed this strategy time and time again and we believe it is the only way to successfully design and build a project. Of course, as we get into the construction phase, I'm talking with my contractor. He has, at times, 200 or even 300 men working for him out in the field, constructing the building per the design. As a developer, I am not going to be talking to each of those 300 people and asking them individual questions. Rather, I go to my point person for my contractor and ask the questions, which are then communicated to the appropriate people out in the field and adjustments are made as needed.

This is how you should be running your office. Let your front desk person be the team leader. You will be a part of the team that helps orchestrate how everything works, but you should not be the main point person.

Long Delays

Probably the number one complaint of patients about their doctors is the amount of time spent waiting for the doctor. If you truly want to run a patient-centered practice and take care of your patients in the way that you would want to be taken care of, you will understand that making patients wait for more than five or ten minutes shows that you don't value their time.

> **Making patients wait for more than five or 10 minutes shows that you don't value their time.**

As I spoke with doctors about this I quickly realized that the doctors who have been successful for decades understood this principle, and the result was strong patient retention. Their patients adored them. It was these doctors' opinion that anything more than five to ten minutes of waiting means you are putting *your* convenience in front of the convenience of your patients.

As discussed at the beginning of this chapter, the idea of putting yourself last is an important element of the success of your practice. If you make your time the priority, your patients will have to wait longer and longer and, in the end, you will create an office very stressed from the pressure the patients put on your front desk. Eventually, the lack of timeliness not only negatively affects your patients, but also affects your employees.

At the end of the day, this will affect you, and you will have more problems to deal with as more people are unhappy in your life. You'll find you're not successful in the way that you originally planned and desired.

Instruct your front desk person to be in continuous communication with the patient. If the patient has to wait even five minutes, the front desk person should be communicating with him or her, explaining what is going on and how much longer a wait is expected. If the wait is longer than fifteen minutes or stretches out to twenty minutes, the front desk person should offer to reschedule the appointment if that is what the patient wants.

The feedback I've gotten from doctors who do this is that the patients love being treated this way. The patients feel appreciated, respected, and valued. You will have a far easier time of retaining them over the years with this kind of courtesy and professionalism.

Of course, if you are continually making your patients wait more than ten minutes and the front desk is continually offering to reschedule, you need to address developing a better scheduling plan with your staff.

You've probably noticed in this chapter that I've placed a high importance on the idea of retaining your patients. The reason is that a retained patient is far less expensive than a new patient. It costs far more money to acquire a new patient. Why? It requires far more processing of paperwork, filing initial contacts with insurance companies, making copies of the card, etc. All these things have to take place with each new patient. You will also place less stress on your staff by retaining patients rather than forcing them to continually deal with new customers.

> **The reason is that a retained patient is far less expensive than a new patient.**

If you take the approach of a concierge-style service, your patients will need to know what to expect. Of course as they continue to visit your office, these explanations will become less frequent or most likely go away. You can see how each element, from billing to filing to educating, consumes large amounts of your employees' time, time that can be spent doing other things.

Ultimately, your office will become more efficient with a large repeat-patient base. Each employee will have time to do more productive things than handling pieces of paper. One way to look at the costs of all this paper is this: it's estimated that it costs you approximately eighty dollars for staff to process, file, or shred it. When your employees put their hands on a piece of paper it is costing you lots of money. You can avoid that waste by minimizing the amount of processing that your staff needs to do.

When I was talking with Dr. Kenneth Tokita about this topic he shared with me a method he has found successful when starting a practice and getting all of the scheduling right: when he first opens a practice, he schedules his follow-ups one hour apart. Now, of course, those follow-ups don't take an hour, but they allow him and his staff to understand how they were able to get each patient through the process of coming into the office, handling any necessary paperwork, and meeting with the doctor. They then analyze the time that it took for the entire process. They begin to learn where they could pick up time and be more efficient. The doctor learns how to be more efficient with the patient during the visit. This was the program until they could comfortably get a patient through the process and have a firm understanding of what was required.

When they felt they were ready, they would start scheduling their follow-ups every half hour. They would repeat the same process of analyzing the visits and then scheduling accordingly. Eventually they would get the follow-up visits down to fifteen minutes. But if they found that a certain type of patient or certain specific patient took twenty minutes, the next time they booked that type of patient or scheduled that particular patient, they would allow for a half hour slot.

This is how they were able to stay on schedule and not cause the patients to wait more than five or ten minutes at most. Additionally, as the doctor became more experienced in handling patients and anticipating questions, he was able to take what was originally a twenty-minute conversation and bring it down to five to seven minutes. This enabled him to maintain the necessary buffer within the fifteen minute scheduled appointment to handle any unexpected items that may arise, and potentially gives the next patient more time.

Of all the topics discussed in this chapter, one of the most important ideas that you, as a doctor, should understand is that most of your patients are in your office are because they're scared. They're concerned about some part of their health, even if it's an annual checkup. They know in the back of their minds that they may not have eaten as well as they should have or exercised as much as was prescribed. They will be concerned that their health has deteriorated or, as in many cases, they will have an ailment that has brought them to you.

> **Most of your patients are in your office are because they're scared.**

Whatever their reason, you need to remember that one of your primary roles is to help them feel calm. Make them feel comfortable, make them feel that you are there for them and interested in learning with them, and from them. They have come to you because of a problem and are looking to you for help in solving it.

With the Internet and websites like Webmd.com, along with the availability of medical studies, most people now have some idea of what they think might be ailing them before they even walk into your office, and they are concerned. I would encourage you to sit down with the patient. Don't stand and review the charts, but sit down with the patient, look them in the eye, and listen. Assure your patient you are going to do everything within your power to help them with the problem they are having, that you understand how they feel and that you understand why they would be concerned. This goes a long way toward creating a connection; the patient feels secure and assured that they now have an advocate who is highly trained and working to help them solve the problem. You do not want a patient to walk out of your office feeling like they just inconvenienced you and interrupted your busy schedule. You want each patient to feel like they are important to you during the time you interact with them. By doing this, you enable them to relax, feel that they have wisely placed their care in your hands, and that you are fully willing to accept the responsibilities that come along with that.

In the end, it is my hope that the main thread you find throughout this discussion on how to run your practice is the idea of taking care of your patients in such a way that they feel human, they feel valued, and they feel supported. They should feel encouraged that they have a team working for them, to take care of them and, ultimately, that you are running your practice the way that you would want to be taken care of. If you had the problems your patients had, you would not want to wait for forty-five minutes, and you would not want to feel that you are inconveniencing the doctor when you visit him. You would rather feel that you have come to visit a friend who is interested in your well-being and eager to help you solve the problems that you face.

> **You want each patient to feel like they are important to you during the time you interact with them.**

Cash-Only

One of the quickest ways that you can become patient-focused is by creating a cash-only practice. When you run a cash-only practice you can focus on the needs of your patients as opposed to all the encumbering needs you have when dealing with insurance companies. The primary benefit from a cash-only practice is that it puts you in control of your pricing.

No longer will the insurance company decide how much you are worth, but rather your worth will be decided by the market. Who is the market? The market is the patients you see every day, and they are the ones that will decide whether what you are charging them is worth the service you are providing.

One doctor I spoke with on this subject likes to use the analogy of a donut shop. He argues that in a donut shop, quantities of donuts are made and the people who come in to buy them pay a set price. But what if there was a middleman? What if the donut shop wasn't able to set the price for the donuts? What if the customers were part of a group and that group had management, had offices, had bills that it needed to pay, and it included a large amount of people?

This group, comprised of hundreds of people, comes to the donut shop owner one day and says, "We will give you access to all the people that are in our group and will have a directory that points them to you, but instead of you charging them your normal $0.80 for a donut, we will pay you $0.40 for the doughnut. Of course it will cost you $0.30 in administrative fees to bill us for that $0.40. So, at the end of the day you'll receive $0.10 for each donut."

> The market is the patients you see every day.

You can see how this seems almost silly. Yet when it comes to our health, we allow other companies to negotiate how our healthcare will be structured.

A cash-only practice removes the companies between you and the care of your patient. It allows you to be in continuous communication with your patient.

It also removes nearly all billing from your business. No longer are you working with collection agencies or worse, doing the collections yourself. You will not have to outsource your billing anymore, and you won't have to designate an employee to the specific task of billing.

> If you aren't running a patient-centered practice and a cash-only structure, your customer is the insurance company.

The fact is: you are running a business. The question is: who is your customer? To answer this question, figure out who's paying for your services. If you aren't running a patient-centered practice and a cash-only structure, your customer is the insurance company. The insurance company is the one who you have signed contracts with and it is the insurance company that pays you. When you are running a cash-only practice, your patients come in, you provide a service to them, and they pay you for that service. When you sign a contract with an insurance company, your patients come in, you provide a service to them, and then you bill the insurance company for your services. Remember who pays you is who you work for.

Types of Cash-Only

There are three basic types of cash-only structured practices:
1. Concierge
2. Partial billing
3. Per-visit fee

Concierge

A concierge practice is based on a retainer payment system. This type of practice is typically structured so that the patient pays a certain amount each year for which you provide services that aren't typically found in an insurance-driven practice. While every doctor provides varying services, the most common elements in a concierge style practice are the following:

1. Same-day scheduling
2. 24/7 access via email and cell phone
3. Patient-driven visit length

Same-day scheduling can be an effective way of reaching patients that seek continuous access to your services. When your car stops functioning, you call the mechanic. You don't expect the mechanic to tell you that he won't be available to fix your car until next week. Instead, you often will not even call the mechanic, but rather drop the car off and ask them to tend to your car that day, while it's at their business. If you are like most people, you will call them during lunch to find out what the status is on your car and when you can expect your car to be fixed. Of course it's a major inconvenience if your car can't be fixed that day. Most people only have access to one car, and not having that car puts a serious damper on your ability to function.

Keep this in mind when you think about the effectiveness of same-day scheduling for your patients. They have an ailment that's troubling them, something that needs to be fixed in their body, and they don't want to wait a week to be able to access you and get the information they need to solve their problem.

Likewise, giving them 24/7 access to you via email and cell phone assures them that if they have a problem it will be readily treated. This is important. When you have a strong relationship with your patients, you want them to feel better, you want them to feel healthy, and being able to address an issue at the onset of the issue gives you the opportunity to maintain each of your patient's health to the level they seek and you desire.

I've spoken with several doctors that have implemented 24/7 access via email and cell phone. They have all reported to me that it is a rare situation in which this access is abused. In fact, the afternoon I was interviewing a particular doctor on this topic he pointed out that while we spoke (on his cell phone for over an hour), there was not one call during that time. He indicated that this was typical for him, and that it was *not* common for him to receive calls late at night or continually from the same patient. Furthermore, he indicated that, in general, it did not interrupt his life much at all.

> it was *not* common for him to receive calls late at night or continually from the same patient.

There is nothing worse than sitting in a doctor's office and feeling like you are interrupting the doctor from something else he would rather be doing. As we've discussed, because most practices are based on insurance, doctors are driven to create such a high volume of patients that they simply don't have time to spend with the patient. They are most likely already late for their next patient visit and will rush through your visit. They will rush through the next one, too, and so on until the end of the day comes.

Because a concierge service is paid for up front, you can see fewer patients, and you will have more time to tend to the patients you see. This will make you feel more relaxed, as you can focus on the patient sitting in front of you. It will also make the patient feel relaxed as he senses that you are there for him and not thinking about rushing off to the next patient.

Partial Billing

Partial billing is when you charge the insurance company the way you would normally bill them for your visit with the patient, as well as tests or any other services that are coded by the insurance company. But in addition to that, you also provide additional services.

Some of the services could be the same as the ones described in the concierge service. But whatever the actually services are, the services would be over and above what is covered by the insurance companies and for these you bill the patients. Having 24/7 access via email and cell phone may be something worth while to your patients such that they're willing to pay you an additional fee to receive that type of access to you. Likewise, the same-day scheduling could also be an option for those that wish to pay an additional fee.

You can see how this could become a complicated situation, forcing you to decide how to offer your services to some and not to others. It can also become problematic with your staff as they attempt to work with new scheduling parameters. But it is a type of cash-only practice that is operating in the United States, and there are doctors that have been successful at functioning under this payment structure.

Per-Visit Fee

The final of the three typical ways to structure a cash-only practice is to have your patient pay a per-visit fee. While this doesn't encompass all of the access and same-day scheduling and other services that can be captured in a concierge style practice, it does address the patient-driven visit length. For instance, when a new patient calls your staff to schedule an appointment, your staff can describe the length of visit options that you offer. Should the patient desire a fifteen-minute visit with you, the fee would be a certain amount. If the patient chooses to have a twenty-five-minute visit with you, there would be an additional charge. And this continues on to the number of minutes you feel are the most you'd want to spend with a patient. This allows the patient to decide how much time he wants, and to pay you for the time that he spends with you.

If you have an existing practice based on a contract with an insurance company and you've decided that you want to transition to a cash-only practice, it is important that you take care of the patients who no longer want to stay with you because they can't afford to or they want to stay with their insurance company. Whatever the reason, it is important that you find the patient another doctor *and* give your patients enough time to make that adjustment. One doctor I spoke with about this felt that three months was a minimum amount of time to give your patients to find another doctor and to make the transition. But whatever the amount of time you give, make sure that you communicate with other doctors in your area and coordinate with them to take some of the patients who will no longer be with you. This will ensure that your patients continue to receive care. It will also give you the best chance at not having disgruntled patients leaving your practice saying negative things about you in the community.

While those who criticize this business plan argue that a cash-only practice only works for the affluent, in speaking with many doctors on this topic, I have found that they often have more time to volunteer and provide more services to those less fortunate than they had prior to a cash-only practice. You can expect to be able to serve those in the community, even outside of your patient base, because you will have more time to volunteer. All the while, you will be generating the income that you need to run a successful practice.

THINGS *to* REMEMBER

1 Take care of your employees.

2 Track your patients as they come through your practice.

3 Give your vision to your employees and your patients.

4 Give your patients a voice.

5 Have your front desk person be the "concierge" for your patients.

Chapter Seven
MARKETING

Marketing is the lifeline to your success. Your success will be measured by the way the patients you want to attract connect with your message. Think about the way you want to connect with your community. How do you want to be seen by your community?

Ideally, how your community will connect with you will be based on your vision of how your practice will interact with patients. The vision that you spent the time to develop, and have communicated to your employees, needs to be the vision that you communicate to your community. As your practice starts up, you should re-shape this message based on the feedback you receive from your patients.

It might be tempting to sit back and wait for the insurance directories to channel their members to your practice. However, if you are more proactive and effective in your marketing, you will, instead, be able to attract the type of patient you want. This will benefit not only the patient, but also your practice.

While hanging a sign on your building will help draw in general patients, the more specific you can be in describing the type of patient you are looking for by the way you market your practice, the better off you will be. These patients you desire will be drawn to your practice.

While the word "demographics" is batted around frequently when analyzing potential locations, typically it is only used as a way of determining whether the type of patient you're looking for is even in the area that you want to work in. What the demographic report does *not* tell you is how to bring a patient to you, and it certainly is not decisive in assuring you that the "right" patient is going to come into your suite.

> ◆
> **If you are more proactive and effective in your marketing, you will, instead, be able to attract the type of patient you want.**
> ◆

If you have ever been fly fishing, you understand that one of the most challenging situations, you can experience is when you see the fish in the pooled area of a river that you're trying to attract with a certain type of fly. Yet, regardless of what you do or how you present the fly to them, they do not bite. You may try a different fly at this point, or approach from a different angle. You may find that they are not biting because you are standing upstream and they can see you. In this situation, it is possible that by simply moving downstream and working a different area; you'll suddenly find great success. You did not do anything differently other than discover the appropriate way to approach the fish that day on that river.

But what if you never put a fly out? What if you stood by the edge of the river and simply watched the fish swim by, never attempting to learn what they were looking for or presenting anything to them for "feedback" from the fish? Instead you just sat and observed. Certainly, there can be some benefit to this, but ultimately it would be a stroke of sheer luck if you were to actually get a fish.

Let's say that you decide to become a bit more proactive and place a net across the river and collect whatever fish came along—or anything else: a shoe, a piece of floating wood, etc. While you are now at least gathering fish, you also will have to deal with other things and other objects that you are not interested in.

When you rely solely upon the insurance companies to provide your patients, you are putting a net in the river. If you put a sign up without any marketing or any input from insurance companies, you are slightly better off than if you were to sit by the side of the river—but not much!

Neither situation—the insurance company sending people to you, or you doing nothing and hoping for the best—is an ideal situation. The point of this chapter is to encourage you to take a proactive step in assuring the success of your practice. And by successful I mean providing the type of services that your "ideal" patients are looking for, so that these people come through your door. It is through this idyllic match that you can be the most successful. Anything else will be a variation on a less desirable situation. In the world of business, when you have the perfect product lined up with the perfect person for that product, there is no better match.

> When you rely solely upon the insurance companies to provide your patients, you are putting a net in the river.

I can assure you that the topics covered in this chapter have been used by many successful doctors. Of course, not all successful doctors have implemented *everything* discussed here, but in talking with many of them I can tell you that they are glad to use the techniques most appropriate for them. In the end you'll find that the construction phase of your project was easy compared to running your practice and attracting the type of patients you think are the best fit for the services you provide.

There are two realms of marketing examined in this chapter: **online marketing** and **offline marketing**. Online marketing is the new generation of marketing, made available by the Internet. This approach to getting the word out about your services and attracting patients will be discussed first. In the offline marketing section we will discuss how to approach people and connect with them in ways that you cannot online, an important element to draw the types of patients you want into your practice. I've spoken with doctors that have used simple offline marketing approaches and been profitable consistently, over several locations, in six months. This is an amazing feat and yet can be done when you understand how to approach the market that you are trying to capture.

Online Marketing

More than 75 percent of American adults use the Internet every day. And, according to national market research, 81 percent of them report having used the Internet to find health care information for themselves or family members. This is too powerful a tool to ignore. And, if you use it well, it will be more effective and less expensive than other forms of marketing your practice.

Your website will not only be an important tool to attract patients; a well-designed interactive site will also help you retain your patients.

Before we get into the specific details of how online marketing can work for your practice, I want to begin by telling you that I know most of you will not be performing the tasks described in this section. Unless you are an unusually hands-on type of person and have a significant amount of free time or a very big passion for marketing, you would be best served by hiring someone for an hourly wage to perform these tasks.

If you do decide to hire someone the Web can be an excellent source of potential hires. While there are several websites where you can post projects for people to bid on, my favorites are Guru.com and Elance.com. Both sites allow you to post the project, specify the tasks in as much detail as you want, and then submit that project to a specific person or to the general population of either Guru.com or Elance.com, allowing you to receive a broader range of bids from a larger audience. Additionally, you can specify whether you want bids to come solely from a certain country or from around the world. It is an excellent way of drawing upon the global market.

There is really no reason that the person you hire for Web marketing needs to be in the same geographic area you are in. All of the communications you'll have with this person can easily be done via email, and I strongly recommend that you put everything in writing anyway. Email communications can ensure the greatest level of clarity and understanding, as well a strong documentation.

So, if you are going to hire an expert, why should you be knowledgeable about online marketing? There are two reasons: the first is to avoid getting ripped off. The second is to enable you to write specific expectations and details of what you want done on your project.

Even if you do not use Guru.com or Elance.com, having a strong understanding of the fundamentals in both search engine optimization (SEO), and search engine advertising (SEA), will keep you from working with someone who really does not know what they are doing. If you understand the basics, you will be able to quickly discern whether the person you are interacting with has a knowledge and understanding in line with what the experts say makes for a successful online marketing campaign.

Likewise, by clearly understanding what needs to be done, you will be able to communicate to whomever you hire exactly what you expect to be done. Set forth your expectations for online marketing in clear, specific detail. While you may not understand everything, you will at the very least understand the main ways of getting to the goal line.

> **Set forth your expectations for online marketing in clear, specific detail.**

And what is the goal? The goal of online marketing is to drive patients to your website and motivate them to contact you and use your services. It is really as simple as that. While it can become intriguing to get caught up in the different elements of online marketing and the various tactics to get to the goal, it is important to keep in mind what the goal is. The goal is to grow your practice by bringing in the type of patients that you can best serve. Patients you want.

While the details and intricacies of all that needs to be done to successfully accomplish your goal may not be covered in this chapter (I would recommend my friend Howie Jacobson's book *Adwords for Dummies*) the main principles are covered. Some misconceptions are even cleared up along the way. I can assure you that by simply understanding these basics about website and online promotion, you will be far ahead of most people—importantly, competitors who are trying to draw traffic to their website.

As you surely learned when you went through medical school, simple does not necessarily mean easy; this is also true when it comes to online marketing. It is time consuming and requires expertise as well as experience, which is why you'll benefit from working with an expert in this field. Find one with good references and with whom you have a good chemistry and then, using what you'll learn from this chapter, you will be able to make the most of the incredible power of the Internet to build your practice.

Search Engines and the Internet

The majority of searches are done on three main search engines: Google, Yahoo!, and MicrosoftLive. Google accounts far and away for the greatest use—three times more searches than occur on Yahoo!. Yahoo!, in turn, receives about twice as many searches as Microsoft. In the world of search engines, Google is definitely king. But that does not mean you should exclude the other two search engines from your marketing efforts. We are talking about ten billion searches between all three search engines. The fact that Yahoo! may receive three billion of those searches is not insignificant.

Within each search engine there are two main areas. There is what is called the "organic" area and what is called the "pay-per-click" (PPC) area. The organic area is based on the keywords that the search engines have indexed. Similarly, the PPC area is based upon keywords you bid on. When someone uses those keywords, the search engine will display your advertisement. In both cases, you can see that everything revolves around keywords so it is essential to develop a good keyword base to have a successful online marketing campaign.

Search Engine Optimization (SEO)

Search engine optimization (SEO) simply means that your site has been "optimized" so that it will appear on the first page the search engine results (SERP), and high on that page. So how do you (or the experts) do this?

There are three main elements for success in search engine optimization.
- Create search-engine-friendly web pages
- Select the appropriate keywords
- Build links from authoritative and respected websites

Create Search-Engine-Friendly Web Pages

There are three ways of ensuring that you create a search-engine-friendly web page. The first way is by using simple uniform resource locators (URLs). URLs are a series of characters that denote a specific location on the Internet, such as http://www.Google.com, which is Google's URL. Google is a simple URL or domain, and simple is a powerful way of creating a memorable URL. You should keep in mind that the search engines use the URL in part to determine the relevancy of your website to the keywords that are being used for the search.

> ◆
> I recommend that you use a local word in your URL.
> ◆

I recommend that you use a local word in your URL. A good example would be having one that includes the city in which your practice resides.

For instance, if your practice is in Tacoma, Washington, and you run an urgent care facility, you might want to consider a domain like www.TacomaUrgentCare.com. Of course, this particular domain may be taken already, so you will have to try different variations. There are websites and consultants that can help you come up with different ideas for your domain name.

If you can successfully insert your target keywords, you will add a greater relevancy to your website from the search engine's perspective, as well as the perspective of the patient you are trying to attract. If you typed "Tacoma Urgent Care" in the search engine box and the results page shows a website named TacomaUrgentCare.com, you will probably select that particular website.

When you create your domain name, it is best not to use hyphens. Hyphens can be difficult to communicate, so it is better to have the words grouped together. You could imagine what a mouthful the domain "www dot Tacoma dash urgent dash care dot com" would become, not to mention difficult to remember. It would be better to be able to say, "www dot Tacoma Urgent Care dot com." (Most people are familiar enough with the Internet that they understand there are no spaces and you can always indicate that there are no spaces between the words.)

Use a Site Map

The search engines do not wait for you to submit your web page to their index and in fact, it is better for the search engine to come to you. Search engines tend to favor the method of finding your site through links from other websites. This is done with programs called robots or spiders that go through the Internet cataloging the different sites they encounter. When a robot reaches a website, it is programmed to look for a site map. Your site map is a guide for the search engine robot to help it determine how to catalog and index your site. If you don't have a site map, the robot will follow the links on the various pages of your website and try to form its own map.

The robot will never do as good a job as you or an expert can. By creating a site map, you help ensure that you get a higher ranking on the search engine results page.

To ensure that your web pages are search-engine friendly, there are three things you should avoid:

- 100 percent Flash-based websites
- JavaScript
- Frames

Adobe Flash is a group of programs that allow you to both create and read Flash files. It has become popular on websites for its capability to bring animation and a more dynamic feel to a website. The search engines, however, have a difficult time indexing a Flash file. There are lots of technical reasons for this, but the point you should take away is this: it is appropriate to use specific Flash in certain areas of your website, but you do not want to have your entire website based on Flash.

The second thing you should avoid is using JavaScript. JavaScript is a programming language that is trademarked by Sun Microsystems. It was originally designed to make it easier for non-programmers to have some of the qualities of Sun Microsystem's more robust Java language without requiring an intimate knowledge of computer programming. While JavaScript can make a website seem very dynamic, it can be harmful when you are trying to optimize for search engines. Search engines are not good at indexing JavaScript, and typically do not understand it. In addition, you will want to have most of the important keywords at the top part of your web page; if you have a large portion of JavaScript language at the top of your web page, you will not be indexed as favorably and not considered as relevant.

Frames are another element you should avoid. They were popular in the 1990s when Internet speeds were slow. With the proliferation of high-speed Internet, frames have become less and less popular and less and less necessary. While there are technical reasons why the search engines have difficulties with a frames-based web page, it is more important that you simply know that you should avoid using them on your web page. At this point there is really no benefit to using a frames-based web page.

By following these three simple guidelines you will create a web page that is easily indexed by the search engine robots and subsequently considered relevant as they compare the key word phrases.

A strong organic ranking is what you want to strive for. Do everything you can to make your website search-engine friendly so that as content is added (new service offerings, scheduling options, notice of awards you and your staff receive, news stories, staff photos and info, etc.), you will benefit from all the effort spent in developing powerful keyword phrases, creating links to your site and drawing heavy traffic.

Keyword Selection

Keywords are the words a search engine user types into the search box. When you type in words like "medical office space" and click on the Search button, the search engine's program compares the words you entered and with the index it has created. Based on complex algorithms, the program looks at the page found in its index and decides whether it is relevant to the search keywords. It will then order these pages based on how relevant the pages are to the search terms. Most people do not use a single keyword to look for a particular item; they use a few words. These are referred to as keyword phrases and are a better description of what a person uses on a search engine.

Understanding the words a potential patient would use on a search engine to find the services you offer is critical to having a well optimized site. It is helpful to think of this as a two-step process for your target market: researching and buying.

Researching

When you research a topic, you may be unfamiliar with the overall topic and are trying to learn something more. For example, if it is time for you to buy a new car, one of the first things you might do is go online to look for one. Because you decide you want a minivan, you type in the word "minivan" and find there are many manufacturers. Dodge, Pontiac, and Nissan all make minivans and all of them have different specifications which may or may not appeal to you.

As you continue to do your research, you learn about features, like ABS braking. You may want doors that automatically slide open and closed. You may want it to be able to seat seven, or you want to make sure it has run-flat tires. As you develop a list of what is important to you, you begin to narrow the number of minivans you are interested in.

Buying

Initially, you may have looked at twenty different minivans, but by the time you are done, you have narrowed it down to one that meets all your requirements. Specifically, it is a Honda Odyssey with the Touring trim package, and it must be white. This will lead you down a certain road of searching. You may begin to look for dealers in your area that carry that specific model. When you get that specific, you have made the transition from a researcher to a buyer.

A buyer is someone who is very specific in what they are looking for. In this example, the people who have this particular car need to be "findable" if you are going to buy that car from them.

Reaching Your Online Market with Keywords

Keywords have been described to me as a state of mind. It's important to keep this idea in mind when you are determining which keywords to capture.

Now I know, of course, you are not selling a car, but you are selling services and as you market your services, you need to know what your market is looking for. This can be done many different ways, but there are a few helpful tools commonly used to acquire this information.

Wordtracker.com is one of the tools used to find specific keywords. It allows you to find both the general keywords (the researching side of searching), and the specific words or keyword phrases (the buying side of searching). Long keyword phrases that are very specific (such as the example I gave you of "2005 Honda Odyssey touring navigation and white") are considered a "long-tailed keyword phrase."

By using a combination of both short keyword phrases and long-tailed keyword phrases, you will capture the greatest percentage of your target market. You, or the person doing the work for you, will also be able to determine who is being attracted to your website (and who is not) based on how you use those keyword phrases. Worktracker.com's value is not only in showing you different phrase variations that may not occur to you, but also in its capability to show you how many people have searched for those different variations. Another helpful feature of Wordtracker.com is that it will give you a combination of words that are both laterally related to what you are suggesting as well as a thesaurus version of what you are searching for.

Wordtracker.com also enables you to see how many people are looking for the keyword phrases you are considering. If you are considering using something like "healthcare real estate," for example, Wordtracker.com will show you how many people are searching for those keywords. This information enables you to understand what keywords will generate the largest amount of traffic for you. What you should not do is simply discard the keywords that only show two to ten people a day; when you add up all of those keywords it can have a big effect on your traffic.

For instance, if you were to add up ten keywords which Wordtracker.com indicates ten people search for that word each day, you would have an additional one hundred people that would see your link and have the opportunity to click through to your landing page.

Another way you can learn more about your market is by finding companies that are successful in drawing people to their website and seeing what keywords they used to target their market. A good tool for understanding how your competitors' websites are targeting the market is a website called Keywordspy.com.

Keywordspy.com allows you to type in a website URL or type in a keyword, and it will give you the keyword phrase results from the searches. If you type in a URL, it will tell you all the keywords indexed on that site and where the site tends to be positioned on the SERP for that keyword. If you type in a keyword, the results will show you all the websites that use this keyword and where each site is positioned for that keyword.

Once you have found the keywords you want to target, you can go onto Keywordspy.com and see what your competitors are doing. You can also, via Keywordspy.com, go to your competitors' websites and see how they *visually* target your potential market. This gives you insight as to what has been successful for other people and it will help you determine where you might improve upon that.

I am aware that we are getting into some business elements that sound very competitive, and even aggressive. And I can understand that may be a turn-off to those of you that are more interested in practicing medicine. But keeping your head in the sand will not make your practice any stronger. Even though you will most likely hire someone to do this work for you, you will benefit by understanding the value of these resources.

Keeping your head in the sand will not make your practice any stronger.

If you are going to do some of this work yourself, ideally, you are using Wordtracker.com to develop your keyword base and to determine which keywords to focus on. You are confirming those keywords with Keywordspy.com to see what your competitors are doing. By using these tools and understanding some of these basic principles, you will have a strong foundation with which to then start building your links. Building your links is really where the rubber hits the road. The links are what the search engines base the relevance on, which is key to ranking.

Link Building

Links are the fundamental way search engines determine what your site is about and how relevant it is to the indexed keyword phrase. It is not just the link itself that is important. The links need to come from relevant sites. In the case of the keyword "car" you want a site that is considered a relevant site by the search engine for the keyword "car."

You also need sites that are considered to be an authority for the keyword. The search engines look for:

- The age of the site
- How many links are coming into the site from other relevant and authoritative sites
- How long the websites will exist

Page rank, which is a proprietary system developed by Google and included in Google's toolbar, and Alexa.com are excellent sites to help you determine whether a site is authoritative or not.

The search engines determine how old a site is by the date the domain was registered. If it was registered fifteen years ago, then you will be considered a higher authority.

Search engines will also look at the number of links that come into the site. If the website has tens or hundreds or even thousands of links, the search engines will increase the authority assigned this particular site for the keyword "cars" accordingly.

The search engines determine how long a website plans on staying around by looking at the length of time they are registered. You can buy a domain for a minimum of a year. You can also buy up to ten, fifteen, or even twenty years.

The search engines have access to this information and can determine from this information, along with over one hundred other indicators, whether the site is truly an authority on the topic. If it sees that the website is planning on being around for a long time, or has already been around for a long time and it has many links, that page will receive a high PageRank.

What I find interesting about PageRank is that it refers to "page" and not "website." This is something very important to keep in mind. While we as consumers tend to think of all the pages that comprise the Nike website, for example, as "equal," a search engine is concerned about each specific page.

A search engine looks at where each link is pointing. If several links point to the same page, that particular page will have a higher ranking. You want to get one of the top one hundred sites in the SERP for the keyword phrase you are targeting to link to your site. Ideally, you want your website to be the *only* link on that web page because as the number of links increase, the power of your link is proportionally diluted. This is how search engines work.

There are other ways of generating links. One creative way is to write articles about something in your industry and, somewhere on that page, link to your website using keywords in your text. These links are called anchor text. So, if you are an orthopedic surgeon, for example, and want to draw potential patients to your site that are looking for knee replacement, those two specific words would become a hyperlink to a page on your practice's website that details knee replacement options, your expertise, patient testimonials, etc. You might even include a link to a podcast.

A word of caution: you do not want to have the same text around those links, and you do not want to have the same anchor text on several different websites. Search engines consider that to be manipulative and will not consider the link as a relevant. In order to avoid that assessment use different keywords in a different order, with different styles, in order to not trigger the search engine robots to think that you are manipulating your link base.

Another excellent way to build links is to blog. When you blog, readers can link into your articles and then link into your main website or you can have direct links off your blog to different services or products you are promoting. As your blog becomes relevant to the topic, the inbound links to your website will also become relevant and cause your website to be considered an authoritative site. A blog on your website will also cause the site to get crawled more frequently by the search engines.

By having several high-quality links coming into your blog and continuously updating your content, you can successfully draw the attention of the important search engines and that will allow you to be a larger part of the conversation for the keyword phrases you are targeting.

Link building is not complicated in and of itself. It is time consuming, and it does require dedication, which is why you will probably engage an expert to help you with this work.

Search Engine Advertising (SEA)

We've talked about the organic side of a search engine results page. There is also a commercial area, which is found in various parts of the SERP. This area is referred to by many different acronyms, but the two most common are SEA or PPC. They refer to the same area of the SERP and the same concept, and it is similar to that of a newspaper.

In a newspaper there are articles, editorials, crossword puzzles, obituaries, and a variety of other elements deemed interesting to its customer base. There are also advertisements. The ads generate the income needed to continue their operations—it is not your subscription that keeps the newspaper running. The advertisements actually make the paper profitable. Similarly, search engines make their money in the advertising section. So how can you take advantage of that and why would you want to? Let's deal with the why first.

Organic search engine results take time to develop. It takes strategy, it takes effort and it takes time—you should expect it to take at *least* four months before you start seeing significant results.

On the other hand, with PPC or search engine advertising, you can see immediate results. As soon as you finish setting up your campaign, organizing your keywords into ad groups, writing your advertisements and designing your landing pages, you're ready to go. You can set up an account, start your advertising campaign, and your ads will immediately start showing within a few hours of clicking Submit. Right away, you can start attracting visitors to your site.

PPC is also an excellent way to test different ideas. You can try different ways of organizing your landing pages with text, images, prices, or layouts. You can test different text within the ads to discern what attracts the market and what type of market is attracted. This is an excellent way to use PPC, and it is very inexpensive. It may cost you $200 to $300, depending on how long you run the campaign. You can completely control the way you spend your money in your campaign; you're not committed to any contracts, and there is no minimum requirement of expenditures. There is only a nominal fee to set up the account.

The benefits of PPC are that it fills the gap while your website develops traffic, and it can give you immediate results, so you can start generating business faster.

It is also an excellent way to test the market. You can see what kind of interest you get with a few different SEA campaigns and test different markets by using keyword phrases specific to that location.

Advertising on the search engines will allow you to accrue a patient base. Although there is a cost involved, search engine optimization involves costs as well. It takes a lot of time to develop the links to your website, which ultimately cost you money for someone's time (yours, or an expert's), and costs you in lost patient visits. It is wise to budget funds for SEO and SEA, as there should always be someone working on your site and online marketing, even if only for a few hours a month. This expense is well worth it and will pay for itself over and over again. Of course, it is a business deduction at tax time.

Let's talk about how to put an ad together. There are basically four lines to work with. Adwords in Google offers an excellent way of showing you how to write your ads, and is the best place to start.

The first line of your ad is also the line the searcher will click on. Research has shown that if you put the keyword phrase on the top line of your ad you will have a higher click-through rate.

For example, if your target keyword phrase is "dogs," you would put the word "dogs" or "dog" in the top line, or line number one, of your ad. Similarly, if you are targeting the keyword phrase "dog training," you would use "dog training" in line number one.

Line two is your benefit. This is where I see 99 percent of the mistakes that occur when writing ads for search engine advertising. Research has shown that putting the benefit on the second line is critically important. When the person looking for dog training types in "dog training" into the search box on the search engine website, and arrive at the SERP, they will see the keyword phrase "dog training" in the top line of your ad and immediately identify with it because it is the exact phrase they used. The next line *must* connect with them emotionally. You want them to think, "This person gets what I'm trying to do!" You could use something that frustrates dog owners' like, "Never have your shoes torn up again!" or "Learn why your dog will never want to pull you down the street again!" These are emotional benefits.

Line three is different than line two because it gives the reader a feature. So in this case, your third line might say, "150 techniques to solve all of your dog problems." That is a feature, not a benefit, and here is where most people make a mistake when they write their ads. They write features but they don't write benefits. That's the biggest mistake you can make because people do not get converted to sales based on logical reasoning (features). It's the emotional benefit that connects, no matter how technical the topic may be.

In the case of a physical therapist, for instance, you could talk about how your patients will be able to pick up their kids again, or carry groceries and no longer struggle. These can be the emotional benefits that you outline to attract patients. See the difference between saying, "Never struggle with your groceries again," and saying, "Open from 9–5, 7 days a week"?

Nine to five, seven days a week is a feature. Same-day appointments are a feature. These features do not draw an emotional reaction from most people. Telling them they will "Never again wait three days to see the doctor!" is getting *closer* to the emotional connection you are looking for.

The fourth and final line is your URL or web address. The URL is something that you tested—you took my advice and ran some tests to see which URL drew the best response, and now in your ads you'll use that URL, including the "www" part.

I recommend that you work with someone who is knowledgeable in this field to establish the price you will pay per click. The prices control the position of your advertisement on the SERP. You might assume that you want to be in the top spot, but that may or may not be true, depending on the service you are advertising.

> **If your ad is in the number one spot, you will get many more of those casual clicks.**

If you set too low a price the search engine simply won't even show your advertisement, but if you focus on local keywords in your phrases you may find very little competition and the keywords phrases could be very cheap.

It is important to keep in mind that you are in a never-ending auction. A competitor can easily come in and start offering more than you at any point.

If you want to be number one, you are going to pay significantly more than the person who doesn't care about the top spot, someone who is just fine with being number four. Sometimes being number one is really important. But sometimes the number-one slot can be costly without being beneficial. You may find that while your click-through rates will go down if you're number four, your conversion rates will increase.

That said, there are advantages to being in the top spot. You're visible. You're prominent, and because of that most people will click on the first one they see if it's in the vicinity of what they're looking for. But this may not be beneficial to you if your ad id not what they're looking for. If your ad is in the number one spot, you will get many more of those casual clicks. If it's an extremely lucrative market, you may not care if you have to absorb some of those additional clicks. But if it's a market where there's not a lot of room for error and you don't have a big marketing budget, you'll need to be more selective about where you position yourself in the results page. Again, working with an expert in this field who can help you determine where your ad should be (and what it should cost), will be worth the investment.

The landing page is where the searcher ends up when she clicks on your advertisement. This page is very important because it will determine how well you do in "converting" visitors. You have attracted your market with your ad and created an expectation in them. If you meet that expectation on the landing page, you will get a higher conversion rate with the landing page.

As a doctor, your main goal is to get potential patients to call you or to email you. If your pay-per-click visitor provides you with an email address, you have the right to contact them. You can add this to your list for other, specific online marketing blasts. Once you have that potential customer's email address, you can continue to communicate with them to promote yourself and your practice.

Communicating with patients via email is an excellent way of staying in touch, particularly with your patients who have expressed interest in learning more of what you have to offer. Designing a landing page that encourages them to share their email address should be an important consideration. Your landing page should focus like a laser beam on these two items: the ability for patients to call you, and an incentive for them to share their name, phone number, and email address with you.

You'll need to provide an incentive since most people consider their email address part of their private information. In the case of an urgent care doctor I know, he offered 10 percent off flu vaccinations for those site visitors that provided an email address. The patient would receive the coupon via email and bring it in when ready for his flu shot. Most people would be happy to provide their email address for something of similar value.

The Internet and search engines give you powerful ways of reaching your market.

You now have the knowledge to get started on your online marketing yourself, or to select the right individual or company from the large pool of choices to do the work for you. You understand the importance of keywords and links, optimization and advertising. Perhaps you will be writing articles and blogging. You understand the key elements for each of the four lines of an online ad and have written it in such a way that you qualify the person you want to attract yet discourage those you don't.

An attractive, well-optimized site that is kept current adds an element of credibility to your practice and to you as a physician. For some patients, online searching is an essential step to learn more about a physician's background before choosing a specialist or new primary care physician. If you do not have a presence on the Internet, be assured that you are losing patients to your competitors who do.

Offline Marketing

There are many ways to do offline marketing (marketing that does not include the Internet), including: print advertising in newspapers and magazines; a direct-mail campaign to a targeted demographic group within selected ZIP codes; radio and television advertising; flyers and brochures; banners; incentives such as discount coupons tied to a use of services; refrigerator magnets distributed to new residents via area realtors; giving free lectures at your local community senior centers and libraries; writing a Q & A column for the local paper; getting a regular slot on local talk radio; and on and on. The choices are nearly endless. Your budget, your specialty, your geographic area, and your understanding of how to best reach your target audience are the factors that you (and a marketing consultant, if you hire one) will consider.

While all of the above can be highly effective when skillfully implemented, I have found the best way to truly connect with your community, to develop a strong relationship with it, is by going out and interacting with the individuals who are part of the community. This requires not only your time, but also an authentic interest in others. Your interactions with members of your community will be to let people know who you are and that your vision is one that will positively affect the community, not simply to sell your products or your services.

> ◆
> **This requires not only your time, but also an authentic interest in others.**
> ◆

The three most effective ways to do this include your involvement with:

- Local organizations
- Sponsorship of local sports, academic, and charitable groups
- Personal relationships

Organizations

Three organizations that I encourage you to participate in are:

Rotary Club
The Chamber of Commerce
Kiwanis

The Rotary Club is an organization focused on helping develop a network of professional and business acquaintances. It gives you the opportunity to provide humanitarian services to those in your area, and to develop friendships through your local club's events where you'll meet like-minded people. Over time, you will form strong relationships with other business people in your area.

Your local Chamber of Commerce is an organization that is focused on building up the economic success of the community by increasing the visibility of businesses in the community. By joining, you develop relationships with other business people in the community. As a member, you will have the opportunity to work and even market with other businesses in the area, and you'll talk with community leaders as well as elected officials. These are invaluable contacts as you establish and grow your practice.

Kiwanis is another excellent organization, focused on leadership for children. Its goal is to raise a new generation of leaders for the success of our country, states, and local communities. The work they do develops ethical, responsible, and purpose-driven leaders skilled in the art of drawing out the best in those around them. Members work to inspire others to achieve more than they thought they could.

> Be an active participant and strive to make a difference in your community.

There are many organizations that have positive interactions with the community. I encourage you to look at all available resources in your area and pick two or three. Be an active participant and strive to make a difference in your community; in return, you will receive the countless benefits of relationships with other leaders and successful people. Interacting with them gives you the additional benefit of being inspired yourself. As you talk with leaders in the community, as you share ideas with successful business people, you will gain new insights on how to more successfully run your practice.

Sponsorships

Sponsoring local sports and academic teams, and charitable events, is also an important, easy, and inexpensive way of getting your name out in the community and letting the community know that you are genuinely interested in supporting it. Whether it is a Fourth of July event, a softball team, or the local women's club annual fundraiser, by showing your support you show others in the community that you are interested in their success and your community's quality of life. I encourage you to go one step further and not only sponsor the team or event, but also to be present; spend a few hours, watch the team play. Interact with the team. Talk with the coaches. Get to know the parents. As you talk with parents about how well a son or daughter is doing, the parents will want to know more about you and what you do. The fact that you did more than pay for a sign on a fence with your business name on it, and actually participated, will be that much more meaningful to the people you meet. This sets you apart in the minds of the parents (or the participants), from others who do not make that investment of time. So take a few hours and spend the time to interact at the event you sponsor.

Relationships

Ultimately, the foundation of effective marketing is all about forming relationships. Your membership in various organizations is an important part of that and so is meeting people in virtually any setting. When you meet people, be interested in sharing what you do and the services you provide, as well as being honestly interested in their lives. Ask questions about who they are, what they do, where they work, their children's ages, whether they are married, and so on. This is the best way to learn more about the people who may be potential patients (or who will refer friends to you), and to let people find out about you.

> As a savvy businessperson, you will be looking for ways to develop new relationships to expand the world of people who know who you are and are familiar with your services.

Wherever you go, even when you run down to the grocery store, always carry your business cards. As a savvy businessperson, you will be looking for ways to develop new relationships to expand the world of people who know who you are and are familiar with your services. Even during brief interactions such as picking up your dry cleaning, you can gather important information about those around you and benefit from these conversations.

Invariably, as you have these conversations, people will be interested in the services you provide because they will become interested in *you* as a person. They will connect with you because you seem authentic. Make sure that you remember that person's name and share it with your front desk staff. If the person does follow up and call your office, you want your front desk to be prepared. By doing this, you will offer a level of personalized service that will surprise most people. Nowadays, most of us are not accustomed to a doctor's office anticipating our call, being warmly greeted by the front desk staff that seems to expect us.

By taking the time to develop these relationships, you will have a group of people that talk about you, and this kind of word-of-mouth is one of the best forms of marketing. As one doctor put it to me, "It's a way of replicating yourself." This is a powerful result of networking with people in your community.

So, spend a few minutes each day, or a couple hours each week, finding new ways to invest in the community. In speaking with several successful doctors about their practices, I've noticed a consistent thread—they have managed to embed themselves in the community in a positive way by affecting the lives of those around them. I encourage you to do the same.

THINGS *to* REMEMBER

1. Use marketing to attract the type of patients you are looking for.

2. Make the effort to understand the fundamentals of online marketing.

3. Keywords are a door into the mind of an Internet user.

4. Building links is the heart of SEO.

5. Use SEA to fill in the gaps of SEO.

6. Understand the difference between a benefit and a feature.

7. Connect with your community by investing your time and money into the things they find important.

Index

7A, 74–76
24/7 access via email and cell phone, 134
504, 74–76
ADA. *See* American Disability Act (ADA)
advertisements, 144, 154
advertising
   radio, 159
   television, 159
Adwords, 155
AIR. *See* American Industrial Real Estate Association (AIR)
air conditioning, 46
Albert, Dr. Bruce, 5
Alexa.com, 152
algorithms, 148
American Disability Act (ADA), 34, 35
American Industrial Real Estate Association (AIR), 49
appointment, 118
appraisal, 71, 72
appraiser, 72
architect, 82, 91, 101, 111
articles, 154

associates, 117
association fees, 55
attitude, 121
attract patients, 142
authentic, 163
authority, 152
bank
   big, 65
   community, 69
   large, 69
   personal, 69
   small, 65, 67
Bank of America, 68
bank statements, 63, 65
banners, 159
Bawa, DDS, Dr. Harpreet, 5
Bawa, Rantandeep, 5
below-market rent, 27
bidding, 101
bids
   details of, 104–107
big bank, 65
big lenders, 68
billing, 115
   partial, 134, 136
blog, 153

boilerplate language, 50
BOMA. *See* Building Owners and Managers Association (BOMA)
Boureston Companies, The, 7
brainstorming, 48
brochures, 159
broker, 17
   commercial, 19
   residential, 19
   seasoned, 20
brokerage houses, 20, 23
brokerage website, 23
Building Owners and Managers Association (BOMA), 51
build-out, 111
business, 113
business credit cards, 66
business people, 77
businessperson, 113
business taxes, 63, 64, 65
buying, 149
CAM, 55. *See also* common area maintenance fee (CAM)
campaign, 144, 155
cash-only, 132–138
cash-only practice, 132, 133
certificate of occupancy (COO), 98
certified lender, 73
certified lending program (CPL), 73
Chamber of Commerce, 161
change orders, 81, 94
chemistry, 144
Cheng, Dr. John, 5
Chinese, 47, 67
city's inspectors, 110
cliques, 121, 122
coaches, 162
commercial brokers, 19
commercial real estate, 19

commission, 24
commitment letter, 70
common area, 33, 52
common area maintenance fee (CAM), 53, 67
community, 117, 139, 160, 163
   banks, 69
   medical and dental, 77
   senior centers, 159
commute, 26
competition, 118
concierge, 125, 134
concierge-style, 129
conditional lien release, 100
condominiums, 77
connection, 131
consistency, 123
construction, 93–112
   type of, 36
construction drawings, 79–92
construction management, 59
construction management fee, 59
construction phase, 109, 111, 141
contractor, 88, 90, 93–95, 98, 100, 111
contractor's bid, 72
contracts
   hourly, 106
control, 46
convenience, 128
conventional loan, 67
COO. *See* certificate of occupancy (COO)
CPL. *See* certified lending program (CPL)
Craigslist.org, 23
creative loans, 67
crossword puzzles, 154
CT scanners, 103
cut sheets, 83
deadlines, 83

Index

debt service, 67, 68
decisions, 115
delays in escrow, 71–74
demographic report, 140
demographics, 140
dental, 32
   office space, 17
dental community, 77
dental doctors, 31
dentists
   general, 31
design-build, 81, 82
detailed drawings. *See* details
details, 81
developer, 109
donut shop, 132
drawings, 102
editorials, 154
Edwards, Wayne, 5
efficient, 130
electrical and plumbing (MEP), 102
email, 158
email blasts, 18
emotional benefits, 156
emotions, 44
employees, 114, 116, 122
employment agency, 120
environmental report, 71, 72
equipment loan, 66
examination rooms, 84
examining bids, 106
exclusive agreement, 18
fax blasts, 18
features, 156
fee
   common area maintenance. *See* CAM
   construction management, 163
   per-visit, 134, 136
finalled, 98

financial
   burdens, 119
   commitments, 27
   documents, 63
   incentives, 83
   success, 115
financing, 61–78
firing, 122
fixed rate, 75
Flash, 147
flooring systems, 37
flyers, 159
fly fishing, 140
follow-ups, 130
four-ply roof, 38
frames, 147
Franco, Omar, 5
front desk, 125
front desk staff, 163
Fuchs, Dr. Albert, 5
full gross lease, 54
full service gross lease, 54
general dentists, 31
general keywords, 150
general lender, 73
general patients, 139
general program (GP), 73
goal, 143
Google, 144
GP. *See* general program (GP)
greensheet, 103
gross lease, 52
guidelines, 147
gunfights, 124
Harder, DDS, Dr. Richard, 5
healthcare real estate, 150
heating, ventilating, and air conditioning (HVAC), 54
heavy traffic, 148
hold back, 98
holdover, 35

hospital, 14, 115
  near a, 26
hourly contracts, 106
HVAC, 51, 54, 55, 103. *See also* heating, ventilating, and air conditioning (HVAC)
incentives, 114
incentivize, 115
indexed, 144
infraction, 123
inspections, 110–111
inspectors, 98, 111
insurance, 115
insurance companies, 116, 129, 132, 141
insurance payments, 116
interests, 43, 45
Internet, 18, 88, 89, 119, 131, 142, 159
  cataloging, 146
interview, 121
interviews, 70
intuition, 121
Jacobson, Howie, 5, 143
JavaScript, 147
key intersections, 27
keyword phrases, 148, 150
keywords, 144, 148, 149, 150, 155, 156
Keywordspy.com, 151
Kiwanis, 161
landing page, 158
last payment, 97–101
lease, 52
  full gross, 54
  full service gross, 54
  gross, 52
  modified gross, 52, 54
  triple net, 52, 53, 54

lender, 64, 65
  certified, 73
  general, 73
  preferred, 73
lenders
  big, 68
libraries, 159
linear accelerators, 14
linear feet, 105
line of credit, 66
link building, 152–159
links, 148
load factor, 51
loan
  conventional, 67
loan officer, 66
loan-to-value (LTV), 67
local, 145
local organizations, 160
long delays, 128–165
Long keyword phrases, 150
long-tailed keyword phrase, 150
Loopnet.com, 22
low ratio, 28
LTV. *See* loan-to-value (LTV)
mailers, 25
manage construction, 107
marketing, 139–164
  offline, 159–160
  online, 142–144
Master Lease, 27
McCarthy, Ken, 5
mechanical, 102
mechanical, engineering, and plumbing (MEP), 81
medical
  buildings, 25
  community, 77
  condominium, 46

office space, 148
school, 144
studies, 131
MEP. *See* mechanical, engineering, and plumbing (MEP)
metal deck, 37
Microsoft, 144
MicrosoftLive, 144
Miller, DDS, Dr. Todd, 5
millwork, 104
modified gross lease, 52, 54
motivation, 123
Nance, Ed, 5
near a hospital, 26
negotiating, 41
negotiations
real estate, 45
Newmark, Craig, 23
new or old building, 33
newspapers, 24, 119
obituaries, 154
objective data, 49
office space
dental and medical, 17
offline marketing, 141, 159
online, 22
online market, 149–151
online marketing, 141, 142–144
campaign, 143
organic, 144
organic ranking, 148
organic search engine results, 154
organizations, 160
overbook, 103
PageRank, 153
parking, 29
ratio, 30
requirements, 30
parking spots, 29

partial billing, 134, 136
partners, 117
partnerships, 61, 63
patient base, 33
patient-centered practice, 128, 133
patient-driven visit length, 134
patient retention, 114
patients, 114, 117, 123, 131, 143
attract, 142
payment process, 95–96
payment terms, 100, 100–101
"pay-per-click" (PPC), 144
payroll, 66
peers, 88, 91
penetrations, 109
perceptions, 43
personal bank, 69
personal financial statement, 63, 64
personalized service, 163
personal relationships, 160
personal taxes, 63, 64
per-visit fee, 134, 136
physical therapist, 156
planning department, 29
plans, 109, 111
plans and specifications, 72
PLP. *See* preferred lending program (PLP)
plumbing, 46
plywood deck, 37
positions, 45
PPC, 154, 155. *See also* "pay-per-click" (PPC)
practice, 126
cash-only, 133
patient-centered, 133
preferred lender, 73
preferred lending program (PLP), 73

preliminary pricing plan, 72, 83, 87
pre-qualified, 70
price, 157
pricing, 132
problem, 42
professional office, 32
profit sharing, 115
programming meeting, 84
progress, 116
progress invoices, 95
quality of life, 26
radio advertising, 159
real estate, 77
  commercial, 19
real estate negotiations, 45
realistic schedules, 96–97
recognition, 47
references, 144
referrals, 70
refrigerator magnets, 159
relationships, 162
rent commencement, 56
repeat-patient base, 130
requests for clarifications (RFCs), 90
reschedule, 129
researching, 148
residential broker, 19
retail, 30
retail centers, 30
review, 109
RFCs. *See* requests for clarifications (RFCs)
robots, 146
roof, 109
roofing materials, 38
Rotary Club, 160
Sakahara, Ron, 5
same-day scheduling, 134

SBA, 69, 72, 73, 74–76. *See also* Small Business Administration (SBA)
SBA loans, 69
schedule, 80, 82, 115, 118
scheduling options, 148
SEA, 155. *See also* search engine advertising (SEA)
SEA campaigns, 155
search engine advertising (SEA), 143, 154
search-engine friendly, 146, 148
search engine optimization (SEO), 143, 145
search engine results (SERP), 145
search engines, 144, 146, 152, 153, 159
seasoned broker, 20
security, 47
security deposit, 47
senior centers, 159
SEO, 155. *See also* search engine optimization (SEO)
SERP, 154, 156, 157. *See also* search engine results (SERP)
sign, 20, 28, 139
single keyword, 148
single-ply roof, 38
site map, 146
sleep centers, 103
small bank, 65, 67
Small Business Administration (SBA), 68
small business owner, 77
sound-insulated, 36
space plan, 80, 83–87
space planner, 84, 89, 91
space planning, 79–92, 85
specific, 149

specification sheets, 83
specific words, 150
spiders, 146
splitting the difference, 50
sponsorships, 160, 161
St. Joseph Hospital, 13
subcontractor delays, 99
subcontractors, 82, 100, 102, 103
success, 139
Sunshine, Dr. Sam, 5
Sunshine, Steve, 5
tactics, 143
taxes
   business, 63, 64, 65
   personal, 63, 64
tax records, 63
television advertising, 159
tenant improvement allowance, 57
tenant improvement construction, 56
tenant improvements (TIs), 13, 34, 57, 58, 72, 75, 96
three-ply roof, 38
TI allowance, 58. *See also* tenant improvement allowance
time and materials-based, 106
timeliness, 128
timetable, 104
timing, 123
Tokita, Dr. Kenneth, 5, 121, 122, 130
toolbar, 152
triple net lease, 52, 53, 54

turn-key, 107–110
type of construction, 36
underserved area, 28
underwrite, 70
underwriter, 70
underwriting, 73
uniform resource locator (URL), 145
urgent care, 146
   clinics, 31
URL, 157. *See also* uniform resource locator (URL)
utilities, 67
value engineering, 105
variable rate, 75
walkthrough, 98
warranties, 55
warranty, 109
warranty period, 35
waterproof, 36
web address, 157
Webmd.com, 131
web pages, 146
Western philosophy, 66
Western world, 47
women's club, 162
word of mouth, 21
Wordtracker.com, 150
working drawings, 80, 83, 87–88
Worktracker.com, 150
Yahoo!, 144
ZIP codes, 159